The Boy from Hell's Kitchen

John George Michael Gabriel Fleming

Acknowledgements

I call this an enhanced memoir. Everything in it is based on something that really happened. But I've had to create scenarios and invent dialogue. Some real characters have been exaggerated for dramatic effect. The language is rough, but that's the way we talked. In fact, I've left out a lot of the four-letter words to avoid becoming too tedious.

This is also a work of collaboration. There's not a sentence in it that hasn't been shown to others and improved by their suggestions.

First, I want to thank the members of our writers' group: Alberta, Anne, Jeanie, Leon, Mac, Paula, Reid, Ron, Sharon, and Steve. We've been meeting weekly since 2011. These guys have put up with all my bullshit, given me good advice, and encouraged me to keep writing. Many times I've found myself without a chapter to share on Wednesday morning, but the knowledge that they'd all be ready to critique me at 9:30 has pushed me to knock something out. The chapters have been percolating a while, so I usually manage to do it.

Second, I have to thank a number of friends and acquaintances who showed enthusiasm and interest when I mentioned that I was writing about Hell's Kitchen. They made me think there might be a wider audience than just my family.

Third, my friend Thomas Hatfield has been invaluable in helping me with the technology to put together an e-book. His passion for Google and its apps has been contagious. I'm now almost as evangelical about it as he is.

Fourth, Steven Bauer, editor at Hollow Tree Literary Services, read the work and provided insight and suggestions from a valued outside perspective.

Finally, I need to acknowledge the contributions of my wife, Margaret, who is in many ways a co-author of this work. She won't hesitate to tell me if something sounds phony or awkward or irrelevant. She edits my work for consistency and flow, often changing the order of paragraphs, writing transitions for me, suggesting additions and deletions. She can't reproduce my voice, but since she's heard all my stories for the last forty-odd years, she can tell me what I need to say.

Marge's experience as a teacher, professor, and editor of various academic and popular publications has made her a demon on checking for grammar, punctuation, capitalization, attributions, tense sequence, misplaced modifiers, and all the other things English teachers find so fascinating. Mistakes in grammar are deliberate; it's the way we talked in Hell's Kitchen. Mistakes in mechanics are my fault for producing them, but her fault for not catching them.

Without Marge, this book would never have been written, because if I hadn't married her, we wouldn't have had our daughter Alison, whose husband Damien got me started by urging me to tell the Hell's Kitchen story. They and their children are my original audience. I hope the rest of you like it.

Prologue

Your mother is just your mother when you're growing up. You don't think about her as a person. She's just always there. And sometimes babies appear when you're not looking.

My mother, Vera Julia Lindros Fleming, had an interesting life, but not an easy one. She grew up on a dairy farm, so she knew about hard work and dependability. When she was 17, her mother and stepfather were persuaded by a Communist campaign conducted among the Scandinavians in Minnesota to emigrate to Russia and become participating members of a commune. Ma's two older brothers were grown, but her parents took her along.

It didn't work out according to the idealized promotion. Ma remembers all the negatives--traveling across Russia in a boxcar--where her hair once froze to the wall; public restrooms with no toilet paper, where people wiped their asses with their fingers and then smeared the shit on the wall. At one point she got typhoid fever and almost died.

Eventually the family ended up in Finland, her mother's native country. There Ma married a playwright named Onni Wiklund. They had a baby girl, Selma, who died at birth. The marriage didn't last.

Ma returned to the US. In New York she met and married my dad, Michael Fleming. She had six sons with Michael. I was the first, born in 1939, followed by Axel, called Acky, born in 1940, close enough for sibling rivalry. More about this later.

I was named John George Michael Gabriel Fleming, John for Daddy's father, George for Ma's older brother, Michael for Dad, and Gabriel for—who knows?—maybe the archangel. As far as I know, I'm the only one who got four names. Axel was named for Ma's older half-brother. I don't know where he got his middle name, Edward. If he had a saint's name, I didn't know it, and there was nothing saintly about him.

Then there were two babies, Charley and Fred, who died in my mother's arms as infants, both from spinal meningitis.

Richard Robert, known as Richie, was born in 1946. A forceps delivery damaged his brain and gave him a serious case of grand mal epilepsy. I remember Ma holding baby Richie on her lap and rocking him while he had seizure after seizure; sometimes the waves of convulsions would last for hours. Eventually he was more or less stabilized with a potpourri of obscurely named medications. Until he was about thirteen, he was pretty much like the rest of us, but after that the drugs slowly destroyed his mind. Sedated, convulsive, dependent, unable to attend school or work, he gradually slipped into a darker world of his own, my mother rocking her man child on her metaphorical lap for forty-five years.

A couple of years later my last brother was born and named Charley after the earlier one. His middle name was Rudolph, and we all believed he was named for the red-nosed reindeer. He was big—over ten pounds—a robust, healthy, laughing baby. He was the super kid of the family—Richie's opposite. I was his ten-year-old mentor and protector in the house and on the street; I gave him some of the attention Ma and Dad couldn't.

I didn't know I'd had an older half-sister until years later. Now I wonder what kind of person she might have been, what it would have been like to have her in my life. Who would I have been with a sister five years older than me? I also wonder what influence I had on my brothers' lives, and what influence they had on mine.

They're all dead now, my mother, my father, my three younger brothers. So out of my mother's seven children, I'm the only one still alive. I'm over 80 now and in good health, so I may make it a few more years and live long enough to finish this memoir. This story is for my family, but also a journey backward for me to recall Hell's Kitchen and the world we lived in. It's helped me see the joy I didn't think was there.

Contents

Acknowledgements

Prologue

Part 1: The Kitchen

1947-1960 The Terrific Tenement

1947 Culinary Delights

1947 The Salvation Army

1947 The Tub

1948 Making Change at a Stoplight

1948 Going to Minnesota

1948 Family Reunion

1948 Grandma's Outhouse

1948 Grandpa

1948 The Drunken Butterfly

1948 Asthma

1949 The Social Worker

1949 Night Time

1949 A Day at the Welfare Department

1949 Shoes

1949 Air Raid Drill

1949 Christmas

Part 2: The Ingredients

1950 The Robbin' Hoods

1950 Flip or Pitch

1950 Learning the Ropes

1950 Cyclops

1950 Circe's

1950 Drunk

1950 The Entrepreneurs

1950   Storm

1951 The Red Pony

1951 Amnesia

1951 The Coal Cellar

1951 Math Class

1951 The Connoisseurs

1951 The Beach Bag

1951 The Parachute

1951 The Freak Show

1951 The Lead Penny

1951 Waiting for the Dentist

1951 Movies

1951 Chess

Part 3: The Pressure Cooker

1951 Pimples

1951 Retribution

1951 God

1951 The Altar Boys

1952 Upstate

1952 Executive Meeting
1952 Puerto Ricans
1952 Hell's Kitchen Aerodynamics
1952 The Flight from Hell's Kitchen
1952 Sex Education
1952 The Business of the Butts
1952 Baloney and Cheese
1952 The Police Station
1952 The Hospital
1952 The Stage
1952 On the Roof
1952 Castaway
1953 Integration
1953 Automotive Shop
1953 The Suit
1953 Boxing
1953 Booze
1953 The TV
1954 Epilepsy
1954 Subway Initiation
Part 4: The Stew
1955 The Hudson River
1955-1959 Jobs
1955 Big Business

1956 The Block
1956 Driver Education
1956 The Mechanic
1957 T-Shirts and Suits
1957 Lunchtime
1957 Street Fighting
1957 Cruising
1958 Spaghetti
1958 Seduction
1958 The Birthday Present
1958 Union Square
1959 The Dickhead
1959 Ambivalence
1959 Dropped
1959 The Goombahs
1959 Dumped
1959 The Enigma
1959 Unrequited
1960 Saying Goodbye
1960 The Last Supper
1960 Moving Out
1960 Hitting the Road

Part 1: The Kitchen

1947-1960 The Terrific Tenement

Six of us, my mom and dad, me and my three younger brothers, lived in a one-bedroom flat at 525 West 47th St. Apartment 32 was on the second floor of a six-story complex. Our flat, one of ninety-six, had two windows, one facing the center courtyard, the other an airshaft with a view of a brick wall. In the summer we opened the windows—there was no air conditioning. In the winter heat was supplied by a massive interconnected system of steam pipes leading to radiators in each apartment. Residents signaled the need for more heat by banging on the pipes, an early form of social networking.

The popping and snapping, as the cold pipes turned hot, cracked the plaster around them and opened a highway for the nocturnal army of roaches, that marched from apartment to apartment searching for food, emitting airborne pheromones for swarming and mating, performing their rear bumper copulation, then leaving their time capsules as gifts, as they have been doing for over three hundred million years.

Our flat wasn't a place for visitors. If you opened the front door early in the morning, you'd see wall-to-wall army cots in the living room, and you might have to step over them to get in. Later in the day the cots were folded up and out of the way. In the kitchen a bathtub, with claw feet and a folding metal/porcelain cover, multi-functioned as a table, a communication center, and of course a bathtub. The kitchen window had a discarded orange crate nailed to the ledge, which served as our refrigerator during the winter. In the summer, Ma shopped daily; leftovers were dropped into whatever sauce or stew the old man was cooking.

The rent was $25 a month for most of the years we lived there—from 1944 to 1960. It might have gone up to $35 by the time we left. I don't remember.

In the late 1960's and early 1970's the building became a den for homeless vagrants and drug addicts and was condemned by the City of New York. The New York Police Department focused on the entire neighborhood as a high drug use area. In 1981 our building was bought by a private housing company and rehabilitated. It reopened in 1983, with forty-nine units of approximately 1100 square feet each. Apparently the remodeling combined two previous apartments into one, and they sold for over 1.5 million dollars each.

Since 2012, Hell's Kitchen has become an art center and restaurant attraction. An apartment rents for $2500 a month or more, and the building I lived in is actually called Terrific Tenements. Residents, often off-Broadway actors and artists, can take the elevator instead of climbing six flights of stairs. The kitchen tubs are probably gone. The street is now tree-lined, and the area is called Clinton. But the name Hell's Kitchen still sticks to the ribs of the devil's old neighborhood.

But back to 525 when I was a kid. The basement was an intricate center of water, steam and electricity. Although most tenants had very little interaction, we were all connected through a complex of the steam pipes, the roaches, and the mumbling voices and loud fights.

Andy Corcus, a retarded assistant janitor, lived in one of the windowless basement storage rooms once used as a coal bin. His job was to feed the demanding furnace beast in response to the incessant hammering of tenants on radiators. I can still see his flaming, sweaty face and the red hot stoking bar striking up the cinders of hell. No wonder he stuttered.

Andy, a big man in his 30s, had a huge cock. Everybody knew it. I don't know how we knew it, but we knew it. The rumor was, disappointed and dispirited women--women with drunken, unemployed, abusive husbands—could go to Andy Corcus's coal room to get their furnaces stoked. His gargantuan cock and the stream of drunken women going in and out were an urban legend. Irrespective of fact, his cock continued to grow in the dark coal room, attracting women, angering husbands, and frightening children. Our biggest fear was that Andy's name and his hot stoking bar would be brought up in reference to our own mothers or sisters.

1947 Culinary Delights

No refrigerator, just an orange crate set in our kitchen window. Milk froze in the winter and went sour during the summer. Our timing had to be exact.

My mother--we called her the pressure cooker queen--would purchase the cheapest, driest, end-cut pork chops she could find and flip them into a pressure cooker with a cup of water, hopefully some potatoes and carrots—no seasoning. That was up to us. We all hated pork chops, and I still do. But nevertheless, when the chops hit the plates and the plates hit the table, the forks flew–no seconds, no leftovers.

Richie's expertise was sandwiches. He would grab two slices of Wonder Bread and throw a chop between them---no salt, no seasoning, just like my mother. As he got older he developed a more efficient and economical method, using one slice of Wonder Bread and two slices of baloney. He would carefully lay out the single slice of bread in the correct position, peel one slice of baloney, then another, laying each sacramentally on the Wonder Bread. His half sandwiches were monastic. No cheese, no mustard, no mayonnaise. Nothing. His final ceremonial act would be the folding of the bread and the eating of the baloney host.

My father was the chef and the artist in the family. He was always cooking something up--either spaghetti sauce, various soups, or *pasta e fagioli*, which we called pastafazool. He'd sprinkle diced pieces of chicken or pork into a great cast iron pot, add vegetables, beans, noodles and tomato sauce, all this while humming or singing operatic arias, continually tasting and adding various seasonings, an orchestration of flavors, colors, and smells. His stirring spoon was his conductor's baton. He never passed the pot without making some kind of new improvisation. His old world symphony of colors, textures, and aromas was always present in our flat—we never went hungry.

1947 The Salvation Army

February

Going to Sally's is a blast--all kinds of cheap goodies.

Ma's gone off with baby Richie to look for clothes. Me and Acky and my buddy Pidgy are scouting the aisles to see what the pickin's look like. Sally's smells a little like dirty laundry or maybe my old man's socks, but whatta you expect in a place with a lotta old stuff laying around. Don't get me wrong--this is the place where we find the best junk. And ain't it really all about using stuff up and leaving nothing on the table? Anyway, that's what my old man says, and he knows about shit like that.

So here we are on the trail, passing radios, bikes, BB guns, and a lotta little kid shit like toys. 'Course, there's a truckload of grown-up stuff we ain't interested in.

As usual, Acky's out in front. I say, "Hey, Ack, check this out."

Pidgy says, "Wow, looka how high they piled 'em up in the middle of the floor."

Animals, more than a hundred of 'em. More than over our heads. More than the Bronx Zoo. Elephants, giraffes, pandas and bears. Not like that shit in the Bible where this old guy Noel or something builds this crappy barge and stacks all these animals up to get away from a flood. Wonder why God was such a prick--doing that shit, sinking the world.

Anyway, two kids get ahold of this big bear and are having fun yanking it.

"It's mine--I saw it first." The bigger kid's dragging this bear up the mountain with the littler shit hanging on and laughing as he gets pulled up over the stuffies. Funny, how I wanna jump in and grab the giraffe and get Acky and Pidgy in on it. Me and Acky always liked giraffes. Dunno about Pidgy.

"Mine," says the big punk, pulling and dragging the little punk up the hill.

"Mine," says the shrimp, hanging on to the bear like it was his.

"Candy asses," says Acky. Acky don't like bears since I tossed his offa the roof in a fight. He cried for a week about that, and I got my ass kicked by the old man 'cause some kid ran off with it.

Other kids see and hear the war on the hill and move in and start pushing and shoving. Two more dive into the stuffies pile and wrestle around. The moms start moving in.

"Edward, you come down from there--right this minute."

"Frederick, stop dragging that child."

The kids do a lotta yelling, so they can't hear. One kid raps another on the head with an ostrich. An arm comes off the bear.

"What's going on here?" says Officer Flim Flanagan, the neighborhood cop. That's not the flatfoot's real name, but we call him that. Acky hides behind the toy counter 'cause this cop don't like his skinny ass.

I say, "We ain't doing nothing."

The cop goes off to pick on another kid for a bigger crime.

Pidgy says, "Let's get down to business and head for the music section."

Over to Ma now. As usual, she's doing her gold mining in the discount rag section, digging with one hand for Sally's deal of the day. Baby Richie is hanging on her chest like a crab on a piling.

"Mum-uh, Mum-uh."

"There, there, I'll put you down for a minute." She lays him on the rag pile and he starts giggling and crawling through the clothes. "Keep an eye on him, will you, Johnny."

"Aw, Maaaa. He's gonna have one of his fits."

"No he isn't. I just gave him his medicine."

She holds up this old orange and green shirt that looks like a pumpkin. "Now look at that," she says. You can wear this with your new pants."

"The corduroy knickers? I hate those faggy pants."

Pidgy says, "My ma wants me to wear knickers too--she says all the kids wear 'em. They're the latest rage."

I say, "Why's the Sally's rag pile the only place you see 'em?"

"Dunno, maybe the kids around here don't wanna wear knickers."

"They look like shit."

"Googie says they're rich kid pants."

"Whaddya mean?"

"Their fathers plays golf in 'em."

"Where'd you see that?"

"In the subway ads."

"They have ads for knickers?"

Pidgy says, "Usually there's some old guy with a golf club smoking a Camel. Did you know that they cost more cause you gotta buy special socks with 'em? By the way, Limeys call girls' panties knickers. Another reason for wearing knickers is to keep your pants from getting caught in your bike chain...oh, yeah, we need to check out the bikes."

Once you get Pidgy going on something, he goes on and on.

Acky gives us a yell. "Looka what I found." He holds this catcher's mitt. Then he opens his fly. I see his little dick.

"Jesus, you have no drawers."

"Pidgy says, "What if you get killed or shot by some cop? Your mother will be embarrassed."

"I forgot," says Acky as he tries to stuff the mitt in his pants and close the zipper. No luck.

"Holy Moly," says Pidgy, "Find an outfielder's glove. It'll fit around your little thing better."

Ma don't pay us no attention. She's going nutsy, diving in and outta the rag bin. Baby Richie's got a T-shirt on his head, and he's grabbing at a hat. I hope he don't have him one of those one-hour fits. Women are reaching around Ma, diving, fighting, and grabbing, looking for stuff the others got their hands on.

The Salvation Army--I dunno why they call it an army--they don't sell guns; they don't have bazookas or tanks. Pidgy says it has something to do with religion, but I don't see no crosses or holy water splashing around.

The great thing about Sally's is the ser-en-di-pi-ty. My teacher, Mrs. Ramsbottom, says that fancy word is like when you go around places and find good shit where you don't expect it. Sorta like running around in a candy store and you have a whole quarter to spend.

"Over there," says Pidgy. "Radios and things."

"Sports," says Acky.

"Wow! An RCA windup Victrola--just what we need," says Pidgy.

Acky says, "Nobody wantsta listen to music."

I say, "You like 'The Lone Ranger' and 'The Green Hornet' on the radio, doncha?"

"What's the Long Ranger got to do with it?"

"They both start off with music to get 'em goin'. Ta-dum, ta-dum, ta-dum-dum-dum. Ta-dum, ta-dum, ta-dum-dum-dum."

"Then buy a radio."

"I already got us some records for the Victrola," says Pidgy. "Ravel's 'Bolero' and some others."

I say, "How we gonna buy it?"

"Maybe you can fit the Victrola in your pants?" says Acky.

"Very funny."

"Hey," says Acky, "Looka the bike--it's a 1931 La Salle."

I say, "Maybe they'll let you take it out for a test ride."

"It's a girl's bike."

"No, it ain't."

Officer Flim Flanagan appears. "I heard what you said about putting things in your pants. What you got in there, sonny?"

It must be shit, 'cause that's how Acky's face looks. He sure is scared of cops.

1947 The Tub

October

Me and Pidgy are on the tub listening to the radio and the hoofbeats of the great horse Silver. Acky's locked in the toilet for doing some shit Ma don't like. This fat voice comes outta the radio and is booming into our face--like when we yell into an empty garbage can.

> *In the early days of the western United States, a masked man and an Indian rode the plains, searching for truth and justice--*

I turn the sound up.

The old man says, "Turn the radio down."

Ma says, "Axel--stop banging on the door."

> *Return with us now to those thrilling days of yesteryear, when from out of the past come the thundering hoof beats of the great horse Silver! "Hi Yo, Silver!" The Lone Ranger rides again!*

Feet and hands are going to it on the metal lids, and the noise bounces around in the tub like a African jungle drum. Ta-dum, ta-dum, ta-dum-dum-dum.

"Stop that banging. Lower the radio," says my old man.

"OK, Daddy." I make like I'm turning it down.

"Lemme out," says Acky, still pounding on the door.

I say to Pidgy, "These guys ain't no Robin Hoods."

> *Mrs. Dawson is on the way to warn her husband about their plans to ambush the fur traders, and if*

not for a rescue by the Lone Ranger, she might have fallen prey to the outlaws--

"What's he mean by prey?"

Pidgy's great, like carrying an answer box around. He says, "Prey's the Road Runner when Wile E. Coyote catches it."

"He never catches it."

"Well, if he did, it'd be prey."

I say, "Remember when Skinny the Blink bought himself that dumb Lone Ranger mask and hat and shit?"

"Yeah, yeah, screw Skinny."

A storm war is brewing on the plains. Ta-dum, ta-dum, ta-dum-dum-dum. Pidgy and me is kickin' real hard now. Can't help it. Lid paint is flying. Acky's pounding on the door. Splinters.

Daddy says, "What the hell's with all that noise. Stop banging on the tub."

"OK, okaaaayy." But we can't stop. Silver's thundering hoofbeats has us on the run.

"I'll come over there and drop the lids on your bony asses." Daddy loves the Lone Ranger–we all love the Lone Ranger.

"OK, Daddy." I turn it down. It's not the same.

"The Lone Ranger is the cat's ass," says Pidgy.

The radio voice booms.

Only 15 cents plus a boxtop-

Pidgy has that sucker look in his eye. I say, "Don't do it."

> *You'll see brilliant flashes of light in the inky darkness inside the atom chamber. These frenzied vivid flashes are caused by the released energy of atoms.*

I say, "Your skin'll fall off."

> *We guarantee you can wear the KIX Atomic Bomb Ring with complete safety. The atomic materials inside the ring are harmless.*

Pidgy is into science shit and goes freaky over atomic stuff. "I got me a nickel--all we need is a dime more. Maybe we can get the dif changing bottles or something."

I say, "Lotta bullshit. Ginzo got him one and was took-- punched little Artie in the head, and the bomb fell off the ring."

"Ginzo says after that he kept the bomb in his lunch box."

"So? Little Artie's still alive and didn't die of X-rays or Kryptonite or shit like that."

"Artie got a head like a helmet," says Pidgy. "'Member the time he jumped outta his window? He thought he was Superman?"

"Are you kids listening to the radio?"

"We're listening, Daddy."

"Someone's at the door," says Ma. "It's those cute little girls from upstairs."

"Mrs. Fleming? Is Johnny home?"

It's Jenny and her sister. She has her arms full of comics.

"Come on in, girls. The boys are on the tub."

Another ad comes on, and the Lone Ranger is hitting the trail, looking for a new problem. I turn the radio off.

I say, "Hey girls, what's up?"

"We'd like to do some trading." Jenny dumps her comics on the tub and sloshes them around. I notice an original *Whiz* comic book under a bunch of *Archies*. Pidgy sees it too. and he shoves it back under the *Archie* so he has time to think.

Pidgy has a big crush on Jenny ever since she let him kiss her. I kissed her too, but I didn't like it--her mouth felt like kissing a tire tube. Well anyway, Pidgy's got a crush on her and don't wanna cheat her too much, so he needs time to think. 'Course I'm reading all this in his mind, and I don't know if it's true, but it sure looks like it.

I say, "I notice you've got a lotta *Archie* comics." Me and Pidgy hate *Archie* but we need to butter her up to get the *Whiz*. Yeah, I know he's got a crush on her, but this is business.

Jenny says, "I got a *Wonder Woman*, Volume One. I'll trade it for two *Supermans* and that *Captain Marvel.*

She's gotta be crazy. Who wants a *Wonder Woman*?

"Pidgy says, "Volume One?"

"Yes, it's the first."

I say, "But Wonder Woman's a girl."

Pidgy gives me the "Shut your mouth" look.

She says, "I thought you guys were into the comic business."

Pidgy says, "Lemme see." Jenny hands over the comic, and he starts reading and giving the "Humm, humm" like he's interested. "She's right, it's a first issue--says so right in the front."

I say, "But for two *Supermans* and a *Captain Marvel*? That's crazy."

Jenny's sister speaks up for the first time. "One girl is worth two guys any day."

Pidgy says, "It's a deal if you throw in the *Whiz*."

1948 Making Change at a Stoplight

June

The stoplight's just turned red. Acky says, "The guy smoking the cigar." He points at the Cadillac. He's got this dirty rag in one hand and a spray bottle in the other. "I'll get on the one behind him."

I spray water on the cigar smoker's windshield before he can say no, and start wiping with my dirty rag. My clean towel's draped over my shoulder like I'm a sort of a waiter. The window's still streaked with dirt.

He sees the clean towel, smiles at me and says, "Pushy little bastard." He blows some smoke in my face and dumps ash on my shoe. I don't pay no attention, just keep smudging. He reaches around in his pocket. I pull the towel off my shoulder and wait with the spray bottle, ready for action. The light's about to turn green; the cigar smoker's fumbling faster. I can hear the change rattling.

Once I get the quarter, I give him the clean towel job before the light changes. He drives off, shaking his head and laughing.

1948 Going to Minnesota

June

Me and Acky are sitting at the back of the Greyhound bus. Ma's in front of us with Richie. One day of farts, cigars, and gas fumes is too much. Add to that, I'm carsick.

Ma's saved up for years, stashing money in a tin can so we could make us a visit to her family in Cloquet, Minnesota. 'Course she didn't tell Daddy or Acky until she bought the tickets. Money don't spend much time hanging around in our house. Would you believe it, I even put some money in her tin can 'cause I wanted to hear those wolves she's always talking about.

"Are you dreaming again?" Acky's popping his knuckles, one finger at a time. One makes a huge pop.

I give him an elbow. "Stop that." He shows me his teeth and keeps popping. Pain in the ass.

Smoke stacks are putting bad air in the back of the bus. Add in the closed windows and old men cutting the cheese and some guy's smelly cigar, no wonder a guy gets sick. Ever get the heaves so hard your eyeballs pop out?

Well anyway, Ma got me some crackers, and I took me a shit at the last stop, so I'm feeling better. Funny what a good crap can do for you.

Some yokels on the next row start talking about the price of corn and how they ain't getting enough rain and some junk they read in the *Farmer's Almanac*, whatever that is, so I get bored and start dozing on and off, with Acky popping his knuckles so's he can keep me awake. Finally the bus wins out and rocks me to sleep.

I wake up. What the hell was that? I heard on the radio that dreams are short--like one minute. That's bullshit-- this one was like hours.

> *It's nighttime, and I'm in these woods next to a fire, cooking a hot dog. Don't ask me how I got there or how I got ahold of one. So here I am cooking this hot dog, and I hear something running around in the woods. Well, I figure it's wolves 'cause I can see their eyes, all red with the fire--just like how Ma told me. Besides, I can hear one of them howling out there on some hill, just like the Wolfman. Oh, yeah, there's a full moon. So what do I do? Nothing. I just keep cooking that hot dog and thinking that I'm gonna eat it before the wolves get me. Guess what? This big wolf comes out of the dark, and he's looking at me and the hot dog and licking his chops, and I'm thinking how lousy it would be floating around in his belly. So I get this idea and toss the hot dog to the wolf, who snaps it up like he hasn't eaten for years. Then he comes over and sits by the fire and looks at me, and I think he's smiling. Yeah, I know wolves don't smile or sit in front of fires, but this is what my dream tells me. So both me and the wolf cook more hot dogs and eyeball each other while looking at the moon and listening to his buddies.*

Then I'm awake and wondering if I'll see a wolf for real in Minnesota.

"Next stop Chicago-o-o-o."

Leaving Chicago, the Greyhound is swooshing over rolling hills, and the road is a blur. Lotsa green stuff out the window. Little white houses scrunched up with trees and rivers and more green--never seen so much green. My window is open, so I can hear a church bell clanging and see families moving around real slow. It must be Sunday. They're going in--lots of mumbo jumbo and sore knees.

Funny, we probably got us more people in 525's flats than that whole town down there. Wonder if they have movie houses or even watch movies. Daddy says they do a lotta God stuff in little towns. That's why he stood home. Don't like "the God shit and the Minnesota squareheads." 'Sides Ma didn't get him a ticket.

I say, "How much longer to Cloquet?"

Acky says, "Can I have the liverwurst sandwich now?"

"You already ate it yesterday."

Richie don't say anything. He looks kinda funny, like he wants to have him a fit. That would be a mess.

I'm still looking out the window and this river is following us, shooting through the trees and moving fast. I don't see any animals, just lots of birds popping in and out, looking for stuff to eat. Funny how the river follows us up and down the mountains, saying hello. Maybe it'll keep doing it until we get to Cloquet. How does water go uphill? Maybe it's one of those delusions.

Well, anyway, the river gets tired and leaves us flat and goes underground where we don't see it no more, and maybe it's coming up in China, with American fish jumping around. Wonder if the Chinese eat American fish?

1948 Family Reunion

June

Ma's mother, Selma Parry, my grandma, was short and stocky, a typical Finlander. She had three children, Axel by her first husband, Victor Mattson; George and Vera, my ma, by her second, Frank Lindros. Axel was nine years older than Ma, and she always liked him better than George, who was only a couple of years older. Maybe there was some sibling rivalry going on, like with me and Acky.

My grandfather Frank was a Swede born in Finland. He was killed in a bizarre accident when Ma was only four years old. He was driving a wagon when something spooked the horse. It veered off the road and into a ditch, pulling the wagon, which overturned on top of Grandpa. The horse, frantically trying to get away, kicked him in the head and killed him.

Some time in the next thirteen years--we don't know exactly when--my grandma Selma married Abel Oinanen. He was a Finlander, a carpenter, and a farmer, but more interesting, he was a Communist. In 1933 he was recruited by a campaign among the Scandinavians in Minnesota to go to Russia and work on a commune. He and Grandma went and took Ma along. The recruits were promised land ownership, which sounded attractive, but when they got there, they found that their only ownership was as members of the commune. They had to work long hours and were treated like indentured servants.

The family, disillusioned by the Soviet experience, after a year or so relocated briefly to Finland. It was there that Vera met and married Onni Wiklund. She was 19, and he was 34, a playwright. He couldn't have been very successful, or the world would have heard of him--maybe as a Finnish Ibsen. He and Vera had a baby girl, who died at birth. The marriage didn't last, and Vera returned to the United States.

Vera lived in New York for a couple of years. Her folks went back to Minnesota. Then she met Michael Fleming, my dad, at a polka dance hall in Harlem. He must have won her over with his dancing--she thought he was almost as good as Fred Astaire. She was 22 and he was 34 when they were married. There must have been something about older men that attracted her.

Ma hadn't been back to Minnesota since then, so I know she was really happy to see her mother. And Grandma must have been glad to see her and the three grandsons she'd never met. Ma had also lost two babies to spinal meningitis before Richie was born, and although I didn't know it at the time, she was now pregnant with Charley.

The thing I remember best about Grandma is that she always had a pot of coffee cooking on a big iron stove in the kitchen. She and Ma spent a lot of time sitting there, talking in Finnish, drinking coffee and looking after Richie. Acky and I spent most of our time outside with Grandpa, fishing, hunting, and getting the lowdown on what it takes to live off the land.

1948 Grandma's Outhouse

June

Grandma's bathroom is wacko. She calls it an outhouse, probably 'cause it smells so bad and you can't wait to get out. When I use it I have to hold my nose with one hand and wipe my ass with the other. That's pretty tough when you're squatting like a chicken with your legs and feet under you. I don't want to get a splinter in my ass or sit on something that missed the target yesterday.

Speaking of wiping, they don't use toilet paper. I guess it costs too much. You have to tear a page out of the old Sears catalog and use that. Problem is, you have to crumple it up first so you don't scratch up your asshole. So here I am, crumpling up paper, perched like a chicken, holding my breath 'cause I can't hold my nose. By the way, I found that a little spit on it softens it up faster--the paper I mean, not the shit.

On my last visit to the outhouse I heard something moving down there, a snake or maybe a beaver sloshing around. Who wants to get bit in the ass? So after a while I get plugged up 'cause I don't wanna do any more shits in there. So I wait and I wait. Ma gets worried, and Grandma gives me a mix of milk of magnesia and prune juice. Then my ass and my stomach gets to grumbling like it wants to do something. So I run off far back into the deep woods and pull my pants down. Guess what? It comes out like a fire hydrant, and I shit all over my pants and underwear.

Now I have a problem. There's no rivers or water anywhere so I can wash myself. I get most of the crap offa me with sticks and leaves. As for the clothes, I get me a long branch and bundle up my pants and drawers in my shirt, like a hobo. So here I go, balls-ass naked, heading back to Grandma's and thinking about how to explain what I did.

This really sucks. It's starting to get dark. Lots of trees and bushes with things moving around, probably wolves looking for something to eat. Then the noises--sounds like padded feet and sniffing getting closer. Circling. I put my hand on my balls--that's the first thing they'll go for if I try to run--running's the worst thing you can do. I grab some rocks and start throwing them into the trees and yelling. That don't do nothing--just makes them move faster.

Now I'm in this open field--but it's not really a field. Guess what? It's a bog. I get stuck. Scared. I start sinking, feet first, then knees, then up to my ass. I work real hard to crawl out, but I just keep getting in deeper. I'd shit in my pants if I had them on. It's dark now. I can see the stars and red eyes moving around me. The padded feet get closer. The only thing holding them back is my stink.

I start yelling. "Help. Help. I'm getting sucked in." Creepy. Creepy. Going down, down--now I'm up to my shoulders. *This is it. Show's over. Wonder if wolves eat kids' heads.*

"Help, help!"

I see some flashlights blinking through the woods.

"Maaa. Maaa. I'm over here. I'm over here."

I can hear Ma and Grandpa yelling, "Jussi, Jussi." Then my foot finds the bottom. *I'm saved.* I use the stick to push myself up. Lights and voices are coming. I can hear the wolves growling and running away.

1948 Grandpa

June

"We better wash those clothes under the pump," says Grandpa. "Take this bucket and soap. I'll pump, Jussi, and you scrub. Get that scrubbing board in the corner. You'll need that too."

"Why do you call me Jussi, Grandpa?"

"It's Finnish for Johnny. Doesn't your mother ever call you that?"

"She does, but I never knew what it meant. Sometimes she calls me *buska nappa*. What's that?"

Grandpa busts out with this big laugh.

"What's so funny?"

"*Buska nappa* is Finnish for shitpants."

I don't see what's so funny about that.

So far nobody's said much about me getting lost and almost dying in the bog 'cept for Acky, who thinks it's too bad the bog gave me back.

So I'm outside now, and Grandpa is pumping away. He's got these big hands like branches, all twisted up and shiny looking with lots of splotches and veins like rivers. Well anyway, it don't take no time for him to fill up the bucket and put me to work. Everybody knows how to wash clothes, so I won't get into that 'cept for my knuckles getting sore on the scrub board.

Grandpa says, "Why did you go so far into the woods?"

"I had this big dump, and I didn't want anybody to see me."

"Dump?"

"Shit."

"What happened out there?"

Now, here is where a guy hasta keep an eye on his mouth. I could be stuck with the name "Shitpants" forever. But, in any case, like my old man says, "It's always a good idea to get a load off your mind." So I start to tell him the story, how I don't like to sit on toilet seats 'cause of the danger. I don't get into the perching and all the other crapola.

"Did you ever do it in the woods before?"

"There's no woods in New York City. Only maybe Central Park, and you don't do a dump there 'cause of the cops."

"Can I make a suggestion?"

I don't say nothing 'cause he's gonna do it anyway.

"Find yourself a big log laying on the ground and stick your bottom over the other side. Make sure there's a slope away from you."

Great idea, but where is this emergency log waiting for me in the woods?

"I'll remember that, Grandpa."

So, we finish my laundry, and I'm hanging it on a clothesline, and Grandpa's giving me another lecture about what to do when I'm in the woods, specially around bogs.

Suddenly we hear a lotta squawking at the coop. So we go over to see if they're having a party. Feathers and rocks are flying and chickens are jumping. Acky beans one, and it gives a big squawk. He's laughing big time. Acky, not the chicken.

"Stop that." Grandpa looks pissed. He grabs Acky by the back of his shirt and gives him some shakes.

"I didn't do nothing. Lemme go. Lemme go."

He lets him go and brushes out his shirt and fixes his collar "You like eggs, Axel?"

"Yeah, sure I like eggs."

"When hens are scared, they don't lay. You won't be getting eggs tomorrow."

"I didn't mean to hit them--just give them some exercise." Who's Acky shitting? He could bean a cat at fifty feet.

"That's good, but too much exercise is not good for chickens. Besides you can hurt them with rocks."

"Not if I don't hit them."

"You boys like to fish?"

I say, "Sure."

"What's those?" Acky points at the top of the barn where the rain don't get. There are lots of mud balls stuck up there.

"Those are barn swallow nests. You see the holes. That's where they live."

Acky says, "How do they make them?"

"Out of lots of things. Cow manure, straw, mud."

Acky says, "Little shit houses?"

Grandpa laughs. "I guess you could call them that. Well, there's this big walleye I've been trying to catch. I might need some help to get him in the boat."

Wow, must be big fishes there.

"Walleye is the best tasting fish ever."

Acky says, "I don't wanna do any fishing."

Leave it up to Acky to be a killjoy.

* * * * * *

Grandpa points at some trees near the lake. "The boat is over there."

Acky says, "Can't we take a break? What's with all the bugs? I wanna go home."

We've walked for over an hour to get to Grandpa's secret lake. The mosquitoes swarm around like Japanese Zeros. My T-shirt is all sweaty, with splotches of blood where I smudged them.

Wow. There's a big one sucking on my arm, pumping blood. Wham! Another dead Nip.

"Once we get out on the lake, it'll be cooler."

"What about the mosquitoes?"

"There won't be any mosquitoes out on the lake. They live around the shoreline in shallow water."

Grandpa knows a lotta shit and maybe I can learn me something. But, in any case, me and Acky are in a hurry to get out of the woods and away from the Jap hell divers. And, of course there's that giant walleye for me to catch. Wouldn't it be the shits if Acky got him?

* * * * * *

"Axel, you have to stop rocking the boat." Acky's working real hard to get attention. Maybe we should use him for bait.

"No, no, Jussi. Ball the worm up and put the fishhook through him. Leave the tail dangle."

"Which end is the tail?"

"The side that's not looking at you."

I say, "Shit, worms don't have eyes, do they?"

"No, they don't. They have something in their front end that senses the light."

"What's a sense?"

He scratches his head. "That's a tough one." He thinks for a while. "It's like there's a big fish in the lake and you feel it's there, even though you don't see it."

Acky says, "What do they need sense or light for if they just wiggle around under the dirt? Sounds stupid to me."

"Let's get back to the fishing." Grandpa rolls up a small ball of white bread. "Here, put this bread on the end of your hook with the worm. Leave the tail to wiggle."

I do that.

"Now spit on it for good luck." I do that too.

Acky says, "It's all bullshit."

Grandpa says, "Jussi, toss your line over there, just on this side of the weeds. That's where the big guy feeds."

"What about me? All I get is a fishing line with a bobber? How come Johnny gets him a pole?"

I say, "'Cause you're a dipshit and you couldn't catch a fish if he jumped up into your ass."

"Oh, yeah."

"Yeah."

Acky keeps rocking the boat, so there ain't no fish for us today.

1948 The Drunken Butterfly

June

Next day me and Grandpa are back fishing on Island Lake, looking for the big one. We left Acky at the farm. Grandpa thought he was too New York. I thought he was a pain in the ass.

So I got me my pole all set up, and it's nice and quiet, with the lake all glassy. I'm looking at this Island that has trees sticking outta cliffs and there's this eagle flying around looking for a fish, maybe my big one, and we got this cloud of butterflies moving in on us like some kinda blizzard flying around our boat, maybe millions. Never seen nothin' like it. Grandpa says they're called Monarchs and are traveling to Mexico. Some of them flopping around in the water with the fish eating them. I wonder if all this is gonna screw up my chances with the big boy. Jesus, looks like birds got the word too. They start zooming around, grabbing mouthfuls of butterflies. Maybe we're into another dud in the fishing department.

I know you're gonna think I made this shit up, but one of these little guys flutters around Grandpa's beer. Maybe it's the shine of the can or the smell--who knows? He's yellow and black with two feelers sticking outta his face. Grandpa waves him away, but the little guy keeps coming back like he has some kinda brain. The sky is yellow with the others fluttering and running away from the diving birds. But not him. He's got his eye fixed on the beer like there's nothing else in the world.

Grandpa puts the can on the seat and says, "Go ahead and have some."

So, guess what? Lumpy--I'm gonna call him that 'cause it's easier--Lumpy flies around, and I know what he's thinking. Then he lands on the can.

I say, "Since when do butterflies drink beer?"

"I never saw that before."

Lumpy gets his fill, flies off, wobbling a little, and disappears into the butterfly and bird swarm.

Now I know a lot about booze from my old man. Boozers are never satisfied with just one. So I get this idea to put some beer on my fingertip and hold my arm up. Guess what? Lumpy flies outta the swarm and makes a beeline straight for my finger--just like my Pops heading to a bar. I put my finger closer to my eye and see Lumpy's long curled-up schnoz--looks like a fire hose on his face--ugly. Then it snaps out like a whip to suck up the beer drop. *Wow*.

Lumpy keeps coming back to my finger returns while his brothers and sisters are doing their water dance on the lake. I know it's him 'cause he wobbles more than the rest. No shit, this is all really true.

"Well, back to the fish story. Since Acky's not around I finally get this little nibble.

"Don't pull on it, "says Grandpa. "Let him bite and run.

"Yeah, I know all about that stuff."

The bobber just sits. Nothing. So I wait. Even the butterflies are gone now and the sun is going down. I can hear a wolf somewhere on the other side of the lake howling for his dinner. I'm looking at that bobber 'til my eyes dry up. I'm afraid to move it, might scare him away. Nothing.

Grandpa puts down a few more beers and starts dozing off.

"Uh-oh. There he goes. He's nibbling again. Shall I yank on it?"

Grandpa wakes up. "Patience, Jussi. "

I think I got him.

"Not yet. Not yet.

"Do you think it's the big one, Grandpa?"

"OK--NOW."

* * * * * *

We're on our way home. The basket is full of fish. I'm carrying the big one. He's hanging over my shoulder. It's the proudest day of my life. *Can't wait for Acky to see this.*

Grandpa says, "I've been trying to get him for years."

"Good thing you grabbed him with the net when the line broke."

"I never caught such a big fish."

What a great day--Lumpy, the drunken butterfly, and now this fish.

"We'll have to get you out here in the winter next time, Jussi. I'll take you ice fishing."

"What's that?"

"You cut a hole in the ice and drop your line in it."

"And the fish are under there? Aren't they frozen?"

"No. They're able to live under the ice."

"Grandpa? You think the butterflies will make it to Mexico?'

"They do it every year. Thousands of miles, starting from Canada."

"How long do they live?"

"I don't know. Maybe a month?"

"How long does it take to get to Mexico?

"I don't know. Maybe four months. No one butterfly makes the trip. It takes four generations."

"What's that?"

"They all die, and their kids finish the trip."

I guess Lumpy ain't gonna make it. Well, at least he had him a great time on Island Lake.

"What's with all the birds flying around the barn, Grandpa?"

"That's the barn swallows. Something's wrong."

As we get closer to the barn, we can see that the mud houses under the roof are all broken.

Grandpa looks at me and says, "Axel?"

I say, "Acky."

1948 Asthma

July

Out of the woods and back in New York. I'm in bed. Can hardly breathe. Heart banging. *Is this what croaking is like? Maybe if I don't think about it, it'll go away. Our Father who art in heaven, thy kingdom come-- What a lotta crap. He ain't gonna do shit.*

What I need is air--I'm getting dizzy.

Acky says, "You look a little blue. Are you gonna die?"

I say, "Is Ma back yet?"

"She went for an ambulance."

"Where's Richie?"

"She took him with her."

Air won't go in, won't go out. It was the smoke from the old man's cockroach roast. Thousands of them on fire, snapping like popcorn. Him holding the burning newspaper to the ceiling near the pipe where they lived, them falling on the floor, their legless bodies, their shiny underbellies, their eggs, the smoke. I can't breathe.

I start rolling around in the bed. *Better on my side. No, on my back. Maybe I should sit up. Why don't they hurry?*

Like fish on dock sucking, heart beating faster and faster, then slower and slower, then stopping--and stopping--and stopped.

Hail, Mary, full of grace, the lord's with me. Blessed art thou among women. Chest plugged, heart pumping faster and faster.

"Ma's back," says Acky. "Got the ambulance guy with her."

The guy comes over to me and takes my pulse to see if I'm still alive. He gets something out of his bag and puts it on my chest to see what's ticking. Now he starts humming. *What the fuck. I'm dying and he's humming?*

"What's your name, Sonny?"

Ma says, "John." Richie's in her arms, crying.

Acky says, "Is he gonna die?"

"Well, Johnny, it looks like you have a little congestion. We won't need to take you to the hospital. Tell you what--I'll give you a decongestant."

Ma says, "But he looks blue."

"That's just the light in here. He should be fine."

"Don't you see he can't breathe?"

"Maybe you should take him to the clinic and have him checked further."

"But--"

"If it was up to me, I'd take him, but it's not up to me."

"But--"

"Tell you what, give him this pill and he should be fine. It's not as bad as it looks."

1949 The Social Worker

March

It's 10:00 Friday morning. I'm sitting on the bathtub reading a comic book to Richie. Ravel's "Bolero" is playing on the Victrola. Ma is feeding Baby Charley on her lap.

Acky, outta breath, slams the door open, rushes in. "Johnny, Johnny. The radio—you gotta hide the radio. And the Victrola. The social worker is coming."

"Holy shit. Stash everything," I say, running to the radio, unplugging it. "Open the closet, quick. Put some blankets over it. Shit. Shit."

"The toaster. Get the toaster," says Ma. Charley starts crying.

Acky unplugs the toaster "Where you want it?"

"In the closet. Put some towels over it." Charley is now screaming. I say, "Is there anything else?"

Ma says "I don't know. I don't know. I don't think so." Richie grabs Ma's waist and starts crying.

Me and Acky bury the radio and toaster with more blankets.

"Hide the wine bottles," says Ma.

No time. Someone knocks.

"Hello. I'm Jane Innes from the New York City Welfare Department."

I'm standing there like a dope. "Can I come in? The department sent me over to do the quarterly report. It shouldn't take too long." She looks like Cinderella with a clipboard.

"Uh, yeah," I say. "My mom's over there on the cot." *Wow*.

"Mrs. Fleming? Can I ask you a few questions and maybe look around a bit. I'm sorry, I have to do this."

Cinderella holds her pen to the clipboard and smiles at my mother. Baby Charley is blubbering and crying on Ma's lap. Ma says, "OK."

Richie, not crying any more, is jumping from cot to cot, chasing something in his head. Me and Acky are standing guard over the closet.

Cinderella says," Sorry, I have to ask this question. Have you purchased any luxury items recently?" She holds her pen to the clipboard and gives Ma a smile. She looks sorry for us. That's good.

Ma takes hold of Charley and sticks her boob in his face to shut him up. She says, "Luxury?"

Cinderella looks around then writes something on her clipboard. "It looks like everything is fine here."

1949 Night Time

September

Night time. Ma is mumbling her usual shit about how she hates New York, and how the old man's a bum, and he don't wanna work, and how she's up to her neck in kids, and how she hasta squeeze every nickel and stand on welfare lines, and how she wants to move back to Minnesota with farmers and cows and wolves

"Shut up—shut the fuck up," says the old man. Like us, he's trying to sleep, and Ma has been going on for hours. Me ready to jump up at any minute, Richie and Charlie banging their heads against pillows and humming down the noise. Acky's quiet--who knows what the fuck Acky's thinking. I wait for her mumbling to die. *I hate the night.*

She finally conks out. *Now I can sleep.*

"You cocksucking bitch—I'm gonna throw you out the window," yells Mike Monahan in the flat above us.

"Go ahead–kill me, then you'll have to take care of the kids," shouts his wife. I can hear thumping sounds and the crashing of plates and glass. I stick my head under the cushion.

* * * * * * *

"Johnny, Johnny, wake up. Somebody threw something big out the window last night," Acky says.

"Lemme sleep."

"I heard her scream. I think he tossed her out the window." Acky laughs.

"Lemme alone."

"Maybe you should get the cops," Acky's still laughing. Pain in the ass.

"Lemme alone, goddammit. I need me some sleep."

"It's only a big bag of garbage."

I say, "Too fuckin' bad," and put my head under the cushion.

1949 A Day at the Welfare Department

October

The welfare waiting room has twenty social workers attached to desks along the wall. The rest of the room is jam-packed with welfare zombies and their mini-zombies, sitting on bleacher benches, waiting to be called.

"José and Maria Gonzalez," calls out Desk Eighteen.

"Si, Señor."

José drags his chain of four kids behind him. One of the links breaks away and José goes after it. There's some running around. Maria grabs the link, repairs the chain, and drags it to the desk.

"Señor," says Jose. "The check, Señor—I did not get the check."

"Maureen Callahan," says Desk Two. Maureen is a redhead with one kid in her arms, another in hand. She says, "It's about time. You could die of old age in this place." The squirming kid in her arms is trying to get away.

Desk Two says, "If you need more time, I can arrange that for you." He laughs; then he smiles at the kid in her arms and tweaks and wiggles his fingers in its face to get a smile. He don't get one. He and the redhead start mumbling something about the check—some private stuff. She starts crying. So I don't hear any more. Maybe I don't want to.

All day long it goes like this. More parents with their kids, bitching, begging for money from the Desks. It's getting dark outside. The Desks are tired, nasty---maybe they're running outta money. Maybe they wanna go home. Maybe the Desks are robots.

At the end of the room Richie falls over and has one of his fits.

Me and Acky run over and stand by Richie like guards, holding back the crowd while Richie's jerking around--then he does that moaning shit. Embarrassing. More people get into the game—and me and Acky are holding them back and yelling for Ma--and Ma hearing--and Ma handing me Charley--and Ma taking over.

"Outta my way," she says. And puts her hand under his banging head.

Some of the zombies rise up from the bleachers and give advice.

"Put a pencil in his mouth—he'll bite his tongue."

"Should we call an ambulance?"

"Do we need to give him mouth-to-mouth?"

"Is there anything I can do?" says a zombie.

"He'll be all right–this happens every day."

The zombie wants to do something.

"It'll be over in a few minutes. Just let him rest here." Ma holds Richie in her arms and starts humming. Me and Acky put on nasty looks, pushing the poking noses back.

"What's going on? Is someone dying?"

"Get back, Joey—you don't wanna catch that."

Finally, Officer Flim Flanagan pushes through the crowd, his silver badge shining, and says "What's going on here?"

Me and Acky want to get our legs moving, but I'm holding Baby Charley, and we still need to guard Richie.

"My son is sick. He just needs a rest." Richie's fit is over now. So Ma picks him up and puts him on the bench and puts his head on her lap.

Officer Flim Flanagan pitches in with Acky, shoving the crowd back. "Move along with you. The show is over. Get back to your seats." He gives a few nudges, and they get the message. "Is there anything I can do for you, Missus?" Ma says nothing—she's busy with Richie. The cop takes his badge into the crowd, looking for another problem.

Richie sleeps for an hour—he gets up and looks a little wobbly like he was on a bender, but fine. "Can I have a Pepsi?" Now we know for sure he's OK.

* * * * * * *

It's the end of the day and finally we get to Desk Seven. The guy has a wart on his nose.

"Why didn't I get the check?" says Ma. Charley is squirming on her lap.

"Your husband didn't come. We told you last month he needs to come in." We've been in front of this guy before; he's a real pain in the ass. "If you want to get reinstated, you'll need to return with him."

By this time, we've been at the welfare office for over six hours, and the Wart is telling us that we need to come back with the old man. *Good luck to that.*

"But we need the money now." She's a bulldog when it comes to the check. Charley begins to cry. "It's OK, dear.

The nice man is going to give us what we want, and we can go home soon."

We all hang around him like Ma told us. I fiddle with some of his papers. Acky keeps kicking the side of his desk.

"Can't you control your children?" says the Wart. It's getting near closing time, and he keeps looking at the clock. He wants to go home more than he wants my old man. Mom wants the check. The clock ticks. Lots more questions about the old man, and Ma keeps agreeing with everything he says, her head bobbing up and down, his mouth bubbling questions about money.

Since Ma never looks at a clock, and the Wart can't take his eyes off of it, Ma has a better hand.

The lights blink on and off a few times. *Maybe they didn't pay their electric bill.*

The Wart gathers up his papers, puts them in his desk, and locks it.

"Why don't we let it go for one more month. Make sure your husband comes in with you next time. This has been going on for six months—we need to get something done about it."

He tries to look in her face, but she has her head down. Baby Charley is laughing now—giggling and drooling spit. His face shines—we're all happy about the check. We can go home.

1949 Shoes

November

Acky comes home barefoot, cursing out his teacher and telling me about his screwed-up day at school.

He says, "Miss Stumpf points her dipshit finger at me and says, 'Axel, please come up in front of the class.'"

Acky says, " I know there's something bad coming down. She says, 'Don't be foolish. Come up here.'"

"No fuckin' way am I going up there." Acky's face is red.

"She keeps telling me, 'You need to come up here. Don't worry; it's something good.' She always does this to kids. Puts 'em out in front and makes 'em look dumb. I'm not up for that crap again."

"She says, 'All right, dear. Don't move, be stubborn.' I know she won't quit, but my ass is nailed to the desk. Then she says, 'Show them your new shoes, the new shoes I bought for you.' I want to crawl under the desk." His face gets redder.

"Holy shit," I say. "She did that?"

Shoes were a big deal in our family. We used them for playing, avoiding cops, climbing over roofs—you name it. We wore and tore the hell out of them. So when my mom bought a used pair for us at the Salvation Army, they were already holey.

I think of me and Acky cutting out pieces of linoleum and sticking them in our shoes, and the wet, cold snow or rain oozing in, and the squeaking sound that we're coming.

Acky goes on. "Then the bitch says something like, 'Now, children, I bought these shoes for Axel because his old ones were so ragged.' Then some shit about the Bible telling us to put clothes on naked people. And some other crap to show how great she is and how grateful we all should be. I'm so mad I take off the shoes and toss them at her and run outta the room."

Later the old man slapped him around for coming home barefoot and took him to the Salvation Army for another pair of holey shoes. Acky didn't do much school after that and spent a lot of time dodging the truant officer.

1949 Air Raid Drill

December

Mrs. Barnes's class. We're all shook up by the fire alarm.

"Everyone under their desks immediately." Kids scramble and dive under the desks.

Joey says, "Are they gonna drop the bomb on us?"

"Nah, Joey—it's only the duck and cover drill. We done this shit before," says Pimples.

Mrs. Barnes smiles. "Remember, children–duck and cover, arms over your head. Do it."

Most of us are under the desks, our arms over the back of our necks, heads down.

"Teacher, Ron's pulling my panties," says Paula.

"Ron--quit that. Duck and cover."

"Teach, Mac done poked me with a ruler," says Reid.

"Leon got my shoe," says Alberta.

"Mac, put the ruler away. Leon, give her the shoe back. Children, you have to pay attention to the drill."

"Why?" says Steve. "My dad says there ain't no way we can get away from the hydergen bomb—it'll turn all of New York City into a coal bin--a twenty-mile hole in the ground."

"What you know about it?"

"My dad knows all about this stuff, asshole—he's a Marine."

"Steve--language. Do you want me to send you to the principal's office again?"

Teach is still standing up. I wonder why she never gets under her desk.

Jeanie's hand goes up from under the seat in front of me. "I have to go to the bathroom."

1949 Christmas

December

Christmas sucks. Lemme give you an example. Ma buys me and Acky some brand new sport shirts for Christmas. Not a bike or roller skates--nothing like what the other guys are getting. At least it ain't socks.

"Look," she says, "I bought them new from the five-and-dime."

This is a first for new things. She always gets us stuff from the Salvation Army. Oh yeah, I forgot about the new sneakers the old man bought us four years ago, but that's not part of this.

Now, like I said, Christmas for us sucks--all that dipshit stuff, like everybody loves everybody for one day.

And money--it's all about money--and stuff--and more stuff. "Nya, nya, nya, look what I got and you ain't got." The bigger the pile, the better. Like Potsy, for instance. He gets a lotta shit cause his old man is a crooked cop. Does that make Potsy a good guy?

And the music. "All I want for Christmas is my two front teeth." Who gives two shits if some kid is looking for his teeth? And what about "Rudolph, the Red-Nosed Reindeer?" Imagine your old man giving you a middle name like that. Well, you don't have to. My old man gave it to Baby Charley. Charles Rudolph Fleming. Why did he do that? Pops likes the song, and he likes Christmas. So what the fuck--he gives poor defenseless Charley a name that'll follow him into hell. Rudolph? Christmas? Forget about it.

Enough of all that. This story's about sport shirts. Don't know what's so sporty about them. Well, anyway, me and Acky get pushed outta the house 'cause Ma is pissed about us arguing.

"Go outside," she says. "Show your friends your new sport shirts."

"Awww, Ma."

"Awww, Ma. Do we have to?"

All the kids are running around with their bikes and roller skates. Skinny has a Red Ryder BB rifle. Couldn't think of a worse guy getting that. The bastard called us "welfare babies." *Like to shove that rifle up his ass.*

Back to the sport shirts. Me and Acky are in Sal's, and he's buying a big load of candy.

I say, "Where'd you get that money?"

"None of your business."

"You took it outta Ma's purse." I can see from his face that he did.

"I got it changing bottles."

"Ma was missing two dollars. You took it."

"No, I didn't."

"Yes, you did."

"Didn't."

"Did." I'm starting to get pissed off, so I grab him by the shirt to maybe smack him around a bit. He backs away and tears the shirt.

I say, "Look what you did. First you rob Ma and then you tear your shirt." Now he grabs my shirt and tears it right down the front.

He says, "Now you can tell Ma you ripped up your shirt too--you stool pigeon."

Part 2: The Ingredients

1950 The Robbin' Hoods

June

In the 1950s in Manhattan money was scarce--at least on 47th Street. But me and Acky and the boys were always hustling something, cleaning car windows, selling shopping bags, or turning in bottles for change. But we had a problem, no place to store the donuts and candy. So we decided to set up a clubhouse in a vacant room next to Andy Corcus's coal room. The location was so crappy we'd have plenty of privacy.

We rummaged around the neighborhood for broken chairs, and sofas—whatever we could find--things people threw in alleys or left in empty buildings. We found some old lumber and built storage shelves for our supplies. I scrounged up some seascapes at the Salvation Army that gave class to the walls--once we'd scrubbed the coal dust off. Googie found three old cot mattresses and plopped them on the floor in a circle—most of our merry band's grandiose deeds were developed on this circle of mattresses.

Now that we had the decor of the clubhouse spiffy, Pidgy said that we should get our act together.

Since Acky was the most fearless of the hunter-gatherers and was always driving our group to do more, we agreed to put him in charge of that operation. Lenny, who was Acky's right hand man, would be at his side to assist. Googie and Skinny the Blink would back him up with their special skills. Googie was our bad mouth and sometimes useful in planning; Skinny specialized in entertainment and dirty tricks. And Pidgy, our chess-playing intellectual, was into organizing and heavy duty brain work.

* * * * * *

We're having our first meeting in the clubhouse. Acky says, "We're gonna need a name, and a way to stand out."

Skinny says, "What about calling our gang the Royals—wouldn't that be hot shit?"

Googie says, "Let's call it the Royal Screws. Perfect for you, asshole."

"Up your ass and your mother's too," says Skinny.

I say "Stop jerking off. Acky's right. We need a name."

Lenny joins in. "I like Royals—the Royal Flushes?"

Googie says, "No shit."

I say, "How about the Robbin' Hoods? We rip off the rich and give to the poor—that's us, of course."

Acky and Lenny say they love it.

"A kick-ass name–forest green jackets—how about woodsmen's caps with feathers?" says Skinny.

"Put that feather up your ass, and send the cap after it," says Googie.

"Take a leap on a rolling donut."

"Your asshole is a donut waiting for the cream."

Googie goes on. "You'd be perfect for a Merry Band of Assholes. Who's going to be Robin?"

Trying to distract them, I suggest that we take a vote. "Everybody who likes Robbin' Hoods say 'Aye.'"

Quickly Acky, Lenny, and I say, "Aye."

Googie says, "You always do that shit, Bo. It's a setup—you three always vote together."

"That's democracy. And don't call me Bo."

They called me Bo, short for Bowlegs. I was the guy with a leg like a bow. Everywhere I went, the crooked leg went with me. A downward look at my leg would provoke, "What the fuck are you looking at, dummy?" Whenever anyone looked at me straight-on, I would do my crab act, scuttling to the side. Most of my moves were pre-planned. I lived my life in profile. When a direct confrontation was unavoidable, I'd resort to distraction. I'd comb my hair, flip a coin--anything to get their eyes off my crooked leg.

Don't get me wrong; I was probably one of the best runners in the neighborhood, out-maneuvering the fastest cops with my signature leg. There was nothing wrong with me that baggy pants couldn't hide.

Googie continues. "Since we are now so fucking democratic, I have an idea."

"Okay," I say.

"I propose we all collect some shit and eat it."

"Why the fuck don't you shut up and let us get down to business?" says Pidgy.

"Bullshit," says Googie.

The day he fell off the taxi's luggage rack and broke his back was our happiest. His appearance months later in a wheelchair cheered us all up. Now, reassembled by the doctors and out of the chair, he's back, the right side of his body partially paralyzed—one leg dragging, one arm limp and mangled. He moves through the neighborhood, his crutches thrown aside, his claw arm tagged to our shoulders, like a crab, us dragging him, him steering us. We let him stay in front to keep an eye on him. One of the guys asked, "Why would we keep a creep like him in our gang?" I told him, "It's always better to keep the mad dog in front of you."

"Let's hit the bakery. The delivery truck door is still open," says Skinny.

Googie says, "You and your dipshit donuts."

Skinny says, "Wasn't that your mom staggering into Andy's room yesterday?"

Everybody says, "OOOHHH."

I say, "Low blow."

Now Googie's pissed. "Lay off the mother shit, fuckhead."

Everybody says "OOOOHH" again.

Skinny lived in the apartment below us, and we'd had a thing going on for years, usually involving shit. Skinny liked to fill brown paper bags with fecal offerings—he gathered up dog crap, and sometimes he took a shit in the same bag, then tossed it off the roof with the precision of a bombardier. Everyone in the block kept an eye on our roof when Skinny was up there. His sneak attack was the smearing-on-the-doorknob trick. You only got clued in with the smell—but by the time you grabbed the doorknob it was too late.

A year ago I kicked his ass for something--I don't remember what--and the Great Shit War began. Gathering more than his usual collection of crap and stuffing it into a bag, armed for attack, he set the bag on fire, banged on my old man's door, screaming "Fire! Fire!", then ran like hell to a nearby vantage point and watched my pop swing the door open, look at the burning bag, and stomp on it. The shit went flying every which way--most of it on his shoes and pants. I beat the crap out of Skinny for that.

"We need to stock up with some canned goods," Acky says. "Maybe we should go down to 44th Street and raise some cash. "We could visit some fruit stands."

Pidgy says, "Let's keep it straight. Remember what happened to Ginzo?"

"Let's cook up some spaghetti."

The council goes on for another hour and ends up as usual--nothing done. But anyway now we have a name for our merry band--the Robbin' Hoods.

1950 Flip or Pitch

June

The rain has just stopped. Water trickles down along the curb dribbling its way to the Hudson River and the gutter's end.

At the piers, kids dive off a sand barge as ships move out to sea. The cemented city, already drying, has the scrubbed smell of after-rain concrete, drawing people out of their tenements and onto their stoops.

Pidgy says, "Let's pitch."

I say, "Let's flip."

Googie says, "Fuck flipping."

Googie's a 'No' guy ever since he got hisself fucked up falling off the cab's luggage rack. He's twisted like a pretzel after the accident, but he's still the best guy on the block at pitching baseball cards--something to do with the wreck. He'll pitch a card, hopping on his good leg in a half circle, then opening up like an umbrella, then sailing the card with an inside toss to some waiting wall. He's a sure thing. Nobody can get closer. Nobody can beat him. Nobody will play him.

"OK," I say, "Let's pitch." I know Pidgy'll never pitch against Googie.

Pidgy whips out his cards and shuffles them a bit, smiling. I know he has a Johnny Sain in there, and I want it bad. "Nah, let's flip." He winks at me and smiles.

Googie says, "Make up your chickenshit minds--flip or pitch?"

"What's the dif, pitching--flipping?" says Pidgy. Me and Pidgy know better.

Now Skinny the Blink comes into the picture. "Hey, guys, what's up? Where we going? What's happening?"

We don't pay him no attention.

"The big guys are warming up for a dice game?" He blinks fast.

Googie says, "Who gives two shits?"

"OK," I say, "let's flip." So I flip a card, and it comes up heads. "Match me."

Bob Feller is looking up at us. He's on one knee, leaning on his bat, smiling, waiting.

Googie says, "A goddam Cleveland Indian—fuckin' losers." Googie hates matching cards. Like matching coins, there's no skill to it.

Skinny says, "Can I get in?" He pulls a stack of cards out of his pocket and snaps at the rubber band on Yogi Berra's face. He flashes it in our mugs, one at a time.

"Wow. I'll pitch you for that," says Googie.

"Say what? You think I'm nuts--pitch with you?"

"I got a Jackie Robinson. I'll even flip you for it. My Jackie Robinson for your Yogi Berra?"

Bob Feller is still on the deck looking up–smiling and waiting.

1950 Learning the Ropes

July

"I don't wanna go, Daddy."

"You have to."

"But, me and the guys got a game going."

"We need to spend some time together so I can show you the ropes."

"What's the ropes?"

"It's complicated. It's something you have to see."

"But we've got a game lined up."

"Go under your bed and get that last picture you drew."

"I don't wanna—the guys are—"

"John. Go get it."

I'm into drawing sailboats, usually clipper ships with big sails. Most everybody says I'm pretty good.

"Which one?"

"The one with the whale crashing into it and tossing the sailors overboard."

I flip through the folder. "This one?" I copied it from a Classic Comic *Moby Dick*. I hold it up. This guy whatshisname--Abab or Ahab--some shit like that--is tangled up in a buncha rope on the whale's back, and this whale with a big square head crashes into the boat, and a lotta splinters and people are flying in the air. No shit, this's a pretty good picture.

"That's the one," says the old man.

I call him "the old man" or "Pops" on the street and "Daddy" up close--nobody on the block calls their old man "Daddy" unless he wants his ass kicked. Since I'm behind his back now, lemme tell you about my old man. He's the best bullshitter and con man I ever knew, and he does it in five languages.

We move from business to business and bar to bar, in search of who knows what, him the tugboat, and me the dinghy dragging behind him. When Pops drops anchor and talks to people, time is in trouble. Me and my sinking ship are in deep shit.

"Como estás?" says Pops to Tony Tomato.

"Bien, bien," says Tony. That isn't his real name, but we call him that 'cause he's fat and wears a red shirt and a green cap--an idea he dreamed up so he can push his tomatoes.

Now we're into the veggie crowd. Buyers and sellers clogging up the sidewalk. Tony's got this hose and he's spraying water on his boatload of tomatoes. Large black ones, little yellow pears, boxes of red cherry. Tony's the tomato king--except for Jerry the Jew and his horse cart. "Red hot tomatoes—get your red hot tomatoes," says Jerry, as he goes through our block, with his horse leaving a trail of shit balls. But that's another story—back to Tony Tomato.

I can't understand much of what they say after they get to bullshitting in Spanish—all this goes on for a while--Pops yakking away, me tugging at his shirt, him telling me to stop that, and him waving my sinking boat into the face of anybody who'll look.

He holds my hand and steers me through the crowd: "the most red hot deals known to man," "fresh from the farm—tomatoes, cucumbers, lettuce—make a king's salad for the hubby tonight." "We've hit the bottom." " Freshest cheese. Lowest prices."

A raggedy-assed kid slips out of the moving legs and stops us cold. I slide behind Pops. The kid starts giving Pops the hard sell by jamming a shopping bag up in his face. "Hey, mister, you wanna bag?" He has fifty more under his arm.

Pops says, "How much?"

"A nickel."

"Daddy? This kid's trying to screw you." I duck my head back behind Pops, getting outta the way of a fat lady's handbag and her shoe.

"Watch your language; this is business. I'll give you a penny." *Pop's a card.*

"That's my cost. My poor mother is sick. I'm the only one bringing in the money." The kid works up a tear and it streaks down his dirty face. *Great pitch, I gotta remember that one.*

"OK, I'll give you two cents. One for you and one for your mom."

"One for me and one for mom adds up to three cents if you include my cost."

Pops smiles and gives the kid a nickel. The old man loves a con.

"Let's go across the street. Johnny–gimme your hand."

"I'm getting tired. My feet are sore."

"Just a few more places." He stops at Garibaldi's Produce. It's a big stand--has just about everything.

"Nobody is here. Where did the guy go?" says this man with a strawberry nose.

"He just left for a while–some kind of emergency," says an old woman, her body bent like a banana.

"Quit that." My old man don't like me tugging at his shirt.

"Banana Lady says, "There's been some talk about Angelo Garibaldi going out of business."

Jerry the Jew's horse cart moves in across the street, and Trigger's grandma dumps a load and pisses on it.

Banana Lady says. "No wonder Angelo's going outta business." She points at Trigger's shit pile."

Strawberry Nose says, "Who's watching the store?"

The Banana says, "The horse cart business is killing these guys."

My old man rolls up his sleeves and says, "Angelo sent me over to cover for him." He whips out one of Garibaldi's little paper bags and pops it open with a snap. The Nose is hovering over the tomatoes, squeezing and sniffing—not paying attention.

"This lettuce just came in," says Pops to the Banana.

The old lady smiles. "I need two pounds of yellow potatoes, one pound of onions, one bunch of celery."

"Yes, ma'am--looks like you're making potato salad."

"How'd you guess?"

"The eggs in your basket."

"Eggs?"

"Yeah, eggs, potatoes, celery, onions—add that up and you have potato salad."

Now listening, the Nose says, "This guy is Sherlock Holmes."

I can see Pops putting the numbers together in his head. He can't read but he can sure add.

"That'll be twenty-five cents," he says as he bags the mix.

The banana lady says, "It seems to me that it comes to fifteen cents."

"Garibaldi told me to mark it up a bit for myself."

"I make that a forty percent markup," says Strawberry Nose.

"Keep your nose out of this," says Pops.

"I'll come back later," says Banana Lady.

"This is all farm fresh produce—you'll not find anything better anywhere. Look, I'll throw in a free tomato and a head of lettuce," says Pops.

Now, the Banana softens up bit and grabs the biggest melon she can find. Holding it up with two hands, she says, "How about this?"

"You got a deal, lady—but the lettuce and tomato are out." Pops bags up the Banana Lady's order.

"Please don't squeeze the tomatoes," he says to Strawberry Nose. "Pick the ones you want and pay for them."

"OK, Sherlock. But I ain't giving you no markup." Nose hands him the money and walks away, mumbling some shit about Pops being a nobody and a con man.

Pops turns to the next customer. "Step up, ladies and gentlemen. Get your farm-fresh produce—no poison sprays—all natural." He eyes this sexy woman with long black hair cruising by--then he opens his arms like Jesus and throws out his chest, singing "O Sole Mio." He's sure got a good voice. The woman keeps walking by and laughs. Then she stops, turns back, and asks Pops if he delivers. A buncha people crowd around her and Pops. *I dunno who they're looking at. Me? This is all very embarrassing.*

An hour later Garibaldi comes back. Gives us some shit about his kid caught in a fence and a dog chewing on the boy's leg. Pops, of course, gets into bullshitting with him in Italian, something—I think—about kids, dogs, and my sailboat. That one I know for sure, 'cause Pops keeps waving my picture around. Then Pops and Garibaldi start talking cash, and Pops gives him all the money. And for real, finally, f-i-n-a-l-l-y, me and Pops hit the road with a box of fruit and vegetables, and my sinking ship—and not a nickel laid out. Helluva deal.

1950 Cyclops

July

I'm making the rounds with Pops again, and he's showing me more of the ropes. This is the fourth bar we went to, and I'm getting tired.

"Let's go home."

"This'll be the last stop."

Pops leads me down a basement—the place looks like a dark wet cave—tiny lights—like eyes shining–looking. Something's moving around. The little hairs on my neck stand up.

He takes me to a chair and a little table in the corner. "You can keep an eye on the action from the bar. I'll get you a Pepsi."

"Daddy?"

"I'll be right back." Pops goes to the bar.

The bartender's this giant guy with a patch on one eye. There's this yucky jar on the bar in front of him—some scary stuff floating around--looks like hands. I don't like this. *What's with Pops? Bringing me into this wet cave with a one-eyed giant, then sticking me in a corner? I need to take a piss.*

"Hey, Mike. How's it hanging?" says One-Eye to Pops.

"Hanging big and low," says Pops. "Let's give a Pepsi to the kid." Some of the bums are slapping Pops on the back, telling him what a great guy he is.

"Your kid?"

"Yeah, that's Johnny—my oldest."

"Ugly little shit, isn't he?"

"Still watering down your drinks?" says Pops.

"Yeah, I piss in 'em."

Everybody in the bar laughs; one guy takes a sniff. This must be the bar Pops told me about. They call this guy Cyclops, like the sign, 'cause he has one eye. If you need to know more, it's all in a comic book—I think it's called the Odd Sea. It all has something to do with the Greeks and some knucklehead sailing around the world looking to get home. I liked the part about this one-eyed giant who eats dipshit people dumb enough to go into his cave. It all ends when this crew gets Cyclops falling-down drunk, and then they stick a spear in the only eye he's got. Then the poor slob runs round in circles, banging into the cave walls with this thing hanging outta where his eye used to be. Helluva story.

The bar is pretty much full of drunks, mostly guzzling beer. The only light is the beer signs flashing on and off on the cave walls. There's two ladies sitting at one of the small tables. Their faces are decorated with a lotta shit on their eyes and lips. They're drinking outta these fancy glasses with a long handle at the bottom--funny how they hold them with two fingers and a pinky up in the air. Two guys at the bar start eyeing them--maybe the pinky action is a come-on.

Cyclops comes over to me with a Coke in his giant hand. He could squash my head like a peanut.

"My daddy asked for a Pepsi," I say. I want to take that back, but it's too late.

"Same shit, kid--drink it."

"But—but--," I look to Pops at the bar and he don't say nothing. *What the fuck?* Cyclops puts the Coke in front of me. It's already opened.

"Drink it, you little shit." A buncha guys laugh. *This ain't funny.*

"No," I say, "I ain't drinking this shit." Pops just keeps laughing.

Cyclops looks pissed, so he moves his hulk head into my face and lifts his eye patch and there's this big black hole, and I feel like puking.

"Daddy, this fuck is gonna eat me."

Pops laughs. Cyclops laughs. Everybody in the bar laughs. *This is no joke.*

"Take care with your language," says Pops.

So here I am sitting in the corner drinking Coke, which I don't like, watching Pops going around showing my sinking ship to a buncha drunks. One old geezer in a jacket and tie wobbles and falls off his stool. Two guys—the ones that were eying the ladies--pick him up and drag him into a booth next to me. He's mumbling some shit about a girl named Matilda and how she made him a cuckle. What's a cuckle? Some kinda chicken? I'd be mad too, if someone called me that. Anyway, whatever it is, it must be worse than chicken because he sure don't wanna be it.

The two guys prop the drunk on the seat, and he slides and falls under the table. They fish him out by his legs, and a shoe comes off. They put it back on.

"Grab his arms, and we can lay him out on the pool table."

"Cyclops'll get mad. Just prop him up again." They prop him up. One of the guys grabs him by the chin and wiggles his head. "Professor, Professor. Wake up."

"Unhand me, you buffoon," says the professor. He slaps the guy's hand away.

"Can you keep an eye on him, kid?"

"Who, me?"

"Can you just let us know if he falls off the seat again."

"I guess so."

The professor starts to flop over again. One of the guys props him up. "Give us a yell if you need help."

I say, "Uh, okayyy." The two guys angle off to the painted ladies, who are laughing at the show.

I watch Pops runnin' around with my drawing–sticking it in lushes' faces—talking—pointing at me. *Maybe I should duck out to the bathroom.* After four shots he starts singing his "O Sole Mio"--*fuckin' embarrassing.* This goes on for a while. *I'm getting tired of this.*

I start looking at the old professor. He's had a few shots more to wake him up—he's looking better now. He must be over a hundred. He's wearing this jacket made out of corduroy, the same stuff my knickers are. He has these funny patches on the elbows—maybe 'cause he leans on bars and wears holes in them. One eye is glassy; the other is clear.

"What's your name, son?"

"Johnny."

"Coincidence. That's my name too. But they call me 'the professor' in here."

"Are you a real professor?"

"I profess to be."

"Can I ask you a question, then?"

"Sure. What is it?"

"What does 'show me the ropes' really mean?"

"Who said that?"

"My pops."

"Well it may come from boxing, where the ropes define the edge of the ring and the parameters of your life, or it may be a nautical metaphor that means to show a new sailor how to haul and coil and rig ropes."

"I get some of that, but what's a Meta Pour?"

"Metaphor. M-E-T-A-P-H-O-R. It's a figure of speech that compares one thing to another. So 'show you the ropes' means your dad is initiating you into the ways of the world."

"I don't get it."

"It means he wants you to learn things, to help you grow up."

"But I'm growing up on my own."

"It's much like when he takes you to a movie, and you experience life through another character."

"Like how I'm Superman when I read a comic book?"

"That's it exactly. You now have powers to fly in mind and body—you are out of yourself—you can make changes."

"Oh. OK. Can I ask you another question?" *This guy is a wizard.*

"Well, they're not paying me to teach here, but--"

"What's a cuckle? Is it some kinda chicken?"

"Uh, you could call it that. You're interested in language, aren't you, Johnny?"

"Yeah, I guess so."

"Guessing will never get you anywhere. Do you like to read?"

"Yeah. I read every comic book I can get my hands on."

"Did you ever read a real book?"

"Like *Dick and Jane*? I read that in school."

"Well, that isn't exactly what I had in mind, but I suppose it qualifies as a 'real book'--just barely."

He waves to Cyclops to bring him another drink. "You want another coke, Johnny?"

"Make it a Pepsi. Thanks." Loud laughter comes from the bar. Me and the professor are drowned out.

Big Nose says, "There's these three guy parrots looking at this girl parrot--"

"Fuck you and your parrots," says Big Ears.

Cyclops says, "Lenny had a lump in his ear--"

"I once had a girl that talked like a parrot," says Potbelly.

"Did you ever fuck a parrot?"

"No, but I know a guy that sleeps with one."

Cyclops says, "--the lump had a shape like a bell—his doc says--"

"Maybe that's why he has the ringing in his ears."

"Picture Potbelly screwing his parrot, and the bird says, 'I love you—I love you.'"

Back to the professor. "Professor?" I say.

"Yes?"

"Why is everyone in here so shitty?"

"Well, this bar has a reputation for having the ugliest, nastiest bartender in all Manhattan. People come here and pay to get insulted by him." Pops hears this and comes over to the professor's booth.

"Take a look at this," says Pops. He's a bit under the weather. He puts my drawing on the table in front of the professor.

"Have a seat, Mike. Can I refresh your drink?" says the professor, as he eyes my drawing and snaps his fingers at Cyclops. "Garçon, Garçon. Drinks all around." He points at me and Pops.

Cyclops looks pissed 'cause he was on a roll with the boys.

The professor, now looking at my masterpiece, says, "Not a bad replication of the inevitability of Captain Ahab's demise."

Pops says, "Johnny has done some really great drawings."

"Obviously he has talent."

Me and Pops are really impressed with the classy language. This guy knows his stuff. The old guy goes on about this Captain Abab and how he–the captain—don't know the difference between a fish and a mammal and how terrible the book is--all about whales and whale shit and whale blubber. And how only a half a percent of the world ever read the whole thing, and how they are all professors looking into whale excreta.

"What's that?" I say.

He tells me it's a fancy word for shit.

Pops says, "We got one more bar to hit."

"Daddyyy."

"May I come along?" asks the professor.

"Sure." says my old man, probably thinking he can get a few drinks offa him.

1950 Circe's

July

Circe's is next door to the Cyclops dump, so it ain't a long wobble away for the professor. Every once in a while Pops gives him a hand, propping him up and putting him right.

"I gave them the idea," says the professor.

"What idea?" says Pops.

"What?"

"You said you gave them the idea?"

"What idea?

"The idea."

This goes on.

"The names," he says.

"What names?"

He mumbles some crap about Circe and Cyclops and how they are both Greeks and how they're cousins.

Circe's Place. Teresa Brewer's voice bubbles out from a jukebox.

> *Put another nickel in –in the nickelodeon.*
> *All I want is having you and music, music, music.*

God, I love Teresa Brewer. She makes my dick wiggle.

On the sign above the doorway, blinking pink and blue mermaids give the come-on—their boobs flashing and their asses and tails wiggling--it's all supposed to be very horny-looking.

> *I'd do anything for you, anything you want me to--*

No way.

Inside, the wall has a huge picture with a lotta fish and whales and stuff. There's this octopus reaching outta a whirlpool and pulling the boat down into it. All the guys are flying through the air, like my masterpiece, and the boat is going down with all the fish looking up at them—maybe laughing at the dumb asses heading where they ain't supposed to be.

The jukebox keeps pumping it out.

Closer, my dear, come closer--

This place is classy, not a bit like the Cyclops dump. Lots of wrist watches and suits at the bar. Ladies. Sitting together at small tables, whispering--waiting for something.

I climb on a stool in fronta Circe. She blows me away with her blue eyes and golden hair. The professor latches hisself onto the bar and puts his ass on a stool tween me and Pops. Circe says, "Oooh, Mike, is this your little boy? He's so cute." I can feel the heat rising. I'm sure I'm getting red. "What's his name?"

"Johnny."

"Johnny, I can see you're going to grow up to be a handsome man just like your dad. Look—he's blushing."

Shit. Everyone's looking at me.

Pops pulls out my drawing and slides it onto the bar in front of her.

"Oh my," she says, picking it up," it's just like the painting on my wall. Has he had any art classes? He's obviously an artist." She has this voice that hangs around after the words come out.

"No," says Pops. "He does it all on his own." They go on for a long time about my lousy drawing. I don't listen any more. *Maybe I should go invisible. Maybe Pops will get drunk and we can go home.*

Behind the bar, there's this huge tank with lots of stupid-looking fish staring at me like I was something to eat. Why the fuck do fish always stare at you? Someone calls for a drink. Circe gives me one of those "be-right-back" smiles; then she moves off behind the bar like she's on roller skates, and there's this smell of flowers.

"Two beers coming up, Marty. Long Island Iced Tea? Two Long Islands at the end of the bar."

Long Island Iced Tea? The drink looks nasty—a little bit of everything splashed on ice—seven squirts from seven bottles and a shot of Coke for coloring--the sound of bottles and glasses.

"My eyes—they ache," says a bald guy.

Hound-Dog Face, next to him, checks his watch. "Ouch, the wife will be pissed--gotta go home."

Baldy says, "Did you hear what I said? I've been coming to this bar for a year, and I can't take my eyes offa her—she drives me nuts."

Another guy with a blue suit and tie says, "Did you notice how her ass jiggles when she walks?"

Baldy says, "Watch when she bends over to get ice."

"Don't fool yourself--she doesn't even know we're alive," says Blue Suit.

Hound Dog says, "I can't even give my wife a cold, and now, she's making noises about this Oliver guy."

"A three-way?" Baldy seems to be listening now. "Come on--stick around for one more and let's talk about it. "A Zombie for Joe." He does this finger-snapping shit. Circe gives him a smile and looks at Hound Dog. What the hell's a Zombie and a three-way?

"I need to go home," says Hound Dog.

"Have one for the road before you go."

The professor says, "When I was young and working myself through college as a bartender--"

"Save it," says Baldy.

"--that was my favorite drink." The professor slips around on his stool a bit. Me and Pops props him up.

The professor says, "It's a long, tall rum drink and is delicious. It has seven different ingredients, all layered, with the darkest at the bottom."

Circe puts a nickel in the jukebox, smooths her hair, and comes over to Pops with this huge smile, touches his hand on the bar and says, "It's your favorite song, Mike."

Pops, who has this kick-ass smile--and he's probably the best looking guy in the bar--gives her a wink and starts to sing along with Nat King Cole; then she chimes in, all of this while looking each other in the eye. *That's sick.*

> *Mona Lisa, Mona Lisa, men have named you.*
> *You're the lady with the mystic smile--*

Pops is pretty good, but it sucks that everybody is looking at them and me. *God, this is embarrassing.*

Blue Suit says, "Beautiful ass, hair, face, luscious lips. I'd trade my old lady in for her any time."

A wrist watch says, "She's not much—I'd stand my wife up against her any time."

Another wrist watch chimes in, "What about her tits?"

I'm getting bored with all this shit. I wanna go home. The barflies keep buzzing about how Circe is laid out and nasty stuff like sticking their wieners into her.

The Professor is still on his drink, "One ounce of orange juice, one ounce of pineapple juice, one-half ounce of apricot brandy--"

Pops keeps belting out the song--for like maybe the third time.

> *Is it only 'cause you're lonely that they've blamed you?*
> *For that Mona Lisa strangeness in your smile?*

Circe, her elbows on the bar, looking at Pops, is working her eyeballs on him and chipping in with the noise.

> *Do you smile to tempt a lover, Mona Lisa?*
> *Or is this the way to hide a broken heart?"*

Whatta lotta crap.

> *Are you warm, are you real, Mona Lisa?*
> *Or just a cold and lonely lovely work of art?*

Nat King Cole sucks, but my pop's not bad. Circe looks like she wants to drag Pops into a coal cellar. I'm not worried, though. Pops may have a taste for the drink, but he don't play around. 'Least I don't think so.

The professor's still droning on about his Zombie, "--one teaspoon of sugar, two ounces of light rum, one ounce of dark rum, one ounce of lime juice--"

Hound Dog says, "I'm not drinking any more. I'm going home." The guy looks at his watch.

"--blend all ingredients with ice except Bacardi 151 proof rum. Pour into a Collins glass. Float Bacardi 151 proof rum on top. Garnish with a fruit slice, a sprig of mint, and a cherry. Don't drink two."

"Two Zombies," says Baldy. "A round for me and the professor. How about you, Mike?"

Pops says, "I never turn down a free drink."

"Three Zombies coming up."

It looks like I'll be here for a long time.

1950 Drunk

August

"The old man's out, and she's been gone all day," says Acky. He looks up from his comic book. He's sitting on the tub.

"Was she drunk again?"

"Yeah, started early this morning, right after you left." His face is back into Superman.

"Where'd she go?" I'm starting to get pissed off.

"I dunno."

"You check for bottles?"

"Yeah, they were all empty." He laughs at something Superman does.

"How are the kids?" Richie and Charley are sitting on my cot listening to "The Green Hornet" on the radio. "Have they eaten anything?"

"I gave them a bag of potato chips." Acky keeps reading the comic book, and now he starts wiggling his toes and making that cracking sound with the big one. He knows he's pissing me off.

"Jesus Christ, kids can't live offa potato chips."

"There's nothing ready, and I can't cook." The big toe makes a huge snap, and I want to break it off.

"Why the hell didn't you go down to the clubhouse and raid our cupboard?"

"Andy Corcus was there."

"In our clubhouse?"

"No, in the basement."

"So what?"

"Ma was there too."

"In the fucking basement? You seen her going down?"

"I'm not sure." Superman lets go of Acky.

"Either you seen her or you didn't."

"Lemme alone. I saw what I saw."

"I don't want you talking about this kinda shit."

"I didn't say nothing to nobody."

"Did you really see her going down there?"

"You told me not to say nothing."

"You crack your toe one more time, and I'm gonna break the fuckin' thing off."

So he snaps his toe again.

1950 The Entrepreneurs

August

"What makes you boss?" says Acky.

"Yeah," says Googie, "who put you in charge?"

"I've been selling bags for years. If you have a better idea-- do it yourselves."

The Robbin' Hoods' food and candy supply is getting low. So we're having this Round Table meeting about raising money for tonight's celebration. Most of the gang's in the basement, except Hutty, who's still searching out donuts.

"Look," I say, "I put up for the first load of bags, right?"

Nobody answers.

"I do all the running around. Right?"

Nobody answers.

"I collect all the cash and put it in the kitty. Right?"

I know if I keep saying "right" enough times, the guys'll get into the "yes" mode. My old man taught me that.

"I don't like the part about you holding the cash," says Acky.

This pisses me off, but I let it slide.

"How do you make money?" says Skinny.

"We throw it all in a pot, and I get ten percent."

Acky says, "What's that?"

"For every dollar we make, I get a dime."

Acky says, "What for? If you throw it in a pot, it's ours. Sounds like a con job to me."

"I lay out the coin for the bags. Besides, the whole thing is my idea."

"A dime for just standing around and telling us what to do?" says Googie.

Acky starts doing that clicking sucking thing with his mouth, sorta like he has something caught in his teeth. Fuckin' irritating.

"Look, we haven't got any coin in the last two weeks. The food supply is going out. The Robbin' Hoods is gonna go belly up if we don't get our asses in gear."

"We don't need coin--there's plenty of shit just laying around," says Acky.

"Yeah," says Skinny. "Me and Acky can visit a few places and get us all stocked up."

Ginzo says, "Bullshit. It's been two weeks, and you ain't done nothing yet. Like Bo said, we need to make a vestment."

Pidgy says, "An investment."

"That's what I said, 'vestment.'"

"Don't call me Bo."

Googie, who usually got lots to say, is clammed up.

"Whaddya think?" I say to Googie.

"I think the ten percent cut's bullshit."

The 'No' guys are getting out in front.

"Whaddya think of five percent going to the guy that sells the most bags."

Googie clams up again. I got Ginzo, and Googie's thinking. My buddy Pidgy is sitting in the wings, waiting.

Pidgy says, "What's the plan?"

"OK, here it is. I put you guys on different corners, with twenty shopping bags each for starters."

"Who picks the corners?" says Googie.

Acky says, "Can't we sell something else?"

Everything I wanna do, he's against.

"I'll keep twenty bags for myself--maybe I'll sell some when doing my rounds."

"Rounds? What rounds?" says Ginzo.

"Somebody's gotta supervise and collect the money and buy more bags."

"How's about us raising money changing bottles?" says Acky.

I say, "I'm telling you. This bag business could go big time."

"Why don't we rob some fruit and start our own stand-- bags and all?" says Googie.

"You guys sell the first twenty. I collect the cash and buy a hundred more--"

Pidgy moves in. "And we sell the hundred and reinvest."

"What's 'reinvest'?" says Acky.

"Put the coin back into the kitty to buy stuff." *Dumb shit.*

"I knew that." *Yeah, right.*

I say, "We sell the hundred and buy a thousand."

Pidgy says, "We take the money we make from the thousand and buy a million. Now we got the money to buy that furniture we saw at the Salvation Army, and maybe a used TV. I spotted a great big eight-inch one with a magnifying glass."

I say, "Good idea. Now that we're millionaires in the bag business, we branch out into the movie business. Charge guys to watch our TV."

"Yeah," says Ginzo, " We can charge a dime a seat. Maybe sell popcorn and candy."

I say, "We could set up a hot dog stand and sell Pepsis and put all kindsa crap on the hotdogs--like onions and cheese."

Pidgy says, "Once we have it up and running, we can sell the idea to suckers in the next block and get a cut."

"We could be the new A&P supermarket on wheels."

Ginzo says, "We could buy the Salvation Army and start selling shit."

Googie says, "Yeah, right. Then we can buy the building over us and maybe the whole fuckin' block. Why stop there? We keep on going and buy New York City."

"Yeah," says Pidgy. "What about the bags?"

* * * * * * *

We're all on the corner of Thirty-eighth Street and Eighth Avenue. I got an armful of bags and am passing them out to the guys.

I say, "Here's the pitch. 'Red hot bags--ladies and gents, get your red hot shopping bags.'"

"Who the fuck would wanna take ahold of a red hot shopping bag?" says Googie. "Dumb."

"That's only the attention getter. It works real good for the Tomato Man. 'Ladies and gents--why tie up your arms with those little bags? For a dime--'"

"A dime? You got them for a penny each," says Acky.

"Markup. That's what they call it on Wall Street," says Pidgy.

"We can't sell 'em for that--too high," says Googie.

Between Acky and Googie, we'll never get shit done.

Pidgy pitches in. "Start high and work down."

"That's right," says Ginzo. "People are suckers for a deal--even when they're getting screwed."

I say, "'Let me finish the pitch. 'For a dime you can bring home twice as much--for a nickel more we'll throw in another bag.'"

Acky says, "Now you're giving them away."

Pidgy says, "You're making nine cents on the first bag and four cents on the second."

"Maybe we should throw in another bag for the three-armed people," says Googie.

Acky says, "What about the poor octopus people?"

Dumb shit.

I say, "Everybody got the sales pitch down?"

"No."

"Yeah."

"I got it."

"Me too."

"OK--next thing's for me to pick your corners."

Googie says, "Who made you King Shit?"

Acky says, "I'm gonna pick my own corner."

I tell Googie, "You stay here. Lots of traffic."

"I want Thirty-ninth."

"I want Fortieth."

"No, fuckin' way. I want Fortieth,"

"How many bags we got?"

"Twenty each."

"I need more."

* * * * * * *

I've got me a buncha bags and am doing my rounds. My brother's on the corner of Thirty-fifth, and he don't look happy. I'm keeping records on a bag and ready to write it down. "How many?"

"Two."

"Fuckin' two is all?"

"These pricks're all trying to get them for cheap."

"A dime?"

"Nah, fifteen cents."

"I told you a dime--maybe give them two for fifteen cents. What the fuck?"

"Fuck you, fuck them, and fuck your fuckin' bags." The crowd starts steering around us.

I say, "You need to cool it."

"You put me on this fuckin' corner--get outta my face. I'll figure it out for myself."

I walk away, shaking my head.

Acky waves his arms and bags like he's batting off flies. "Shopping bags, red hot shopping bags. Get your red hot fuckin' shopping bags--fifteen cents." The crowd skirts around him, staying outta his reach.

I write down "2" for Acky and head for Googie on Thirty-eighth Street.

Great day for shopping bags. Sunny and cool. Lots of bagless people squeezing and smelling fruits and vegetables. Got me a big order for Tony the Tomato Man for a hundred--'course I hadda lower the price to get the sale.

"Shopping bags--red hot huge shopping bags--ten cents. Cut down on shopping time; do it all today in one big bag. For another nickel you get outta a pickle."

"Are you selling pickles, child?" says an old lady.

"No, ma'am, just bags." I let a few fall outta my arms--she helps me scoop them up, even though she has one of those arm bags with stuff flopping out.

She says, "I'll take two."

"Fifteen cents, Ma'am."

"Child, I thought you said ten cents each?"

I don't like the "child," but the customer is always right.

"That's the pickle I was talkin' about."

"Pickle?"

"I meant you were in a pickle with the small bags and needed a bigger one."

I lay out all my bags on the street and help the lady put her groceries in one of them. I make a big deal outta this--waving arms, talking loud, that attention-getting sorta shit.

I say, "Let me help you put your handbag into the other shopping bag." She doesn't like that--maybe she thinks I'll split with it. More customers crowd around to see the action.

She reaches into her purse and digs around for a long time--she's got a lotta shit in there.

"Here's ten cents, dear. Hold on--I'll see if I can find you another dime. Will you take pennies?"

"A nickel's good."

Jesus Christ, lady--get outta the way.

Customers start picking up the bags and trying to hand them to her--they think she's the bag lady. I grab them all up, and she's still looking for another dime, digging around her in her purse.

"Shopping bags--red hot shopping bags--ten cents. Cut down on shopping time--do it all today in one big bag--for another nickel, you're outta a pickle."

* * * * * * *

After selling a bunch, I put it in the record, then make it over to Googie on Thirty-eighth Street.

Googie's doing his cripple show in high speed today, outta balance and ready to hit the cement any second, then re-screwing himself to start all over again.

"Red hot shopping bags. Red hot shopping bags. Five cents each."

A guy throws a coin in a coffee can next to Googie's sidewalk show.

"Poor kid--no, no, I don't need a bag."

"What the fuck? You're supposed to sell them for a dime each? And what's with the coffee can?"

The sonofabitch has his own business on the side.

"You got more bags? I'm running outta bags."

"Plenty, but none for you."

"Whadda you mean?"

"These aren't nickel bags."

"What's it to you, if I sell a lot for a nickel? Did you ever hear the word volume?"

A customer says, "Hey kid, give me two of those nickel bags." He hands Googie a buck. "Can you make change?"

"Sure." Googie goes into his coffee can.

"I'll take one," says another and drops some extra coin in the can.

I say, "How many'd you sell?"

"All of them--got some of Ginzo's to keep going." He does some more of the hopping and twisting to drum up traffic.

"Where's the money in the can go?"

"To the gang, of course. Thanks, lady. Here's your change."

"How many bags did you sell?" I hold my pencil up, ready to write.

"Dunno--too busy to count. You gonna give me more bags?"

"Fuck, no."

* * * * * * *

Ginzo is sitting on the curb having a smoke and waiting for more bags. I hand him ten more.

I say, "Googie tells me you gave him some of your bags."

"Yeah, business wasn't too good so I lent him some of mine."

"Lent?"

"How come he gets the best corner and I get the shit corner?"

"How many bags did you lend him?" I hold up my accounting bag and put my pencil to it.

"Most of them."

"I need the right number." I tap my pencil on the bag and look him in the eye.

"I got an idea."

"What's with you? How many bags?"

"Why don't we set up a protection business?"

I keep tapping my pencil, trying to get him back on track.

"These fruit stand guys are always getting ripped off, right?" says Ginzo.

"Look, I needa get the number. The other guys are waiting."

"We goes around and tells 'em the Robbin' Hoods are the good guys and we can protect 'em from getting robbed."

"The bags. How many fuckin' bags did you sell?"

"Here comes a customer. Hey, hey, red hot shopping bags--red hot-- Hang on a minute, lady. My buddy just brought in a loada new bags."

* * * * * * *

Pidgy's across the street, talking with one of the fruit and vegetable stand guys. I whistle him over.

I say, "How many did you sell?" I hand him ten more.

"All of them. What's the count?"

"Who the hell knows? Acky's griping and won't tell me shit. Ginzo's cooking up some gangster idea--"

"Damn."

"--and Googie's doing a cripple act with a coffee can."

"What's with the coffee can?"

"He's doing like an organ grinder's monkey. The suckers are throwing coin in this coffee can."

Pidgy laughs at that. "You gotta give it to Googie--he's always looking out for himself."

I say, "I don't think this bag business is gonna work."

"It's just a personnel problem."

I say, "That's right. The help sucks."

"What we need to do is get rid of them and then diversify."

"Huh?"

Pidgy says, "Branch out. Do bigger things. I got me this idea that we connect up with all the fruit stand guys and be suppliers of their shopping bags."

"That's my idea. I already set that up with Tony Tomato."

"We get some of the little guys from the block to work for apples and that sorta shit--they keep an eye out for fruit bandits."

"And help the customer bag their stuff," I say.

"And mark up the the price of the bags."

"Not too high," I say, "Remember we'll be doing it all wholesale."

Pidgy says, "And the profits'll get bigger since there's only the two of us."

"We can get us a truck and go into the tomato business."

"I'll get me a gang on Wall Street and make a zillion. Then I'll buy one of those yachts and sail around the world," says Pidgy.

"What's with all the 'I' shit?"

"I really meant 'we.'"

"But what about the Robbin' Hoods and 'All for one and one for all'?"

"That's the Three Musketeers--a different gang."

1950 Storm

August

"Your move," says Pidgy. The game's been going on for hours. Another dippy day with me getting slaughtered.

A storm's coming in from the west, down by the Hudson. Clouds are boiling around and thunder is cracking away. I'm counting: one...two ...three...four, and "boom." Four miles. It's moving a mile a minute. Should be here in four minutes.

Ah, shit. Here comes Googie and Skinny.

Googie's got this yellow portable radio. It's dumping Frank Sinatra all over the roof. I hate Frankie Boy. Googie's nutso over him. Even combs his hair like Frankie, with little twirly curlies.

"What's up?" says Googie.

Me and Pidgy give them the "don't want you around" look.

Skinny picks up on that and throws us some snot. "Looka the 'tellectuals?"

"In-tellectuals," says Pidgy.

"Yeah, yeah, whatever. What's wrong with checkers?" says Skinny. "I beat a guy three games of checkers once."

"Good for you. You're a real birdbrain."

I say, "You could be a master player with a record like that, birdbrain."

"I ain't no birdbrain, Bo."

Pidgy says, "Better not call him Bo."

I say, "Could you turn off the radio. I wanna hear the thunder moving in."

"Googie says, "What for?"

"Cause I hate fuckin' Frank Sinatra."

Googie sees that I'm pissed off, so he backs down on the radio a bit.

"Fuck you guys," says Skinny.

I say, "Turn the radio off."

Googie by himself is bad enough, but paste him to Skinny and you got a real problem.

"Why don't you guys get your asses off our roof?"

Skinny says, "This is my roof too."

"No, it ain't."

"Yes, it is.

"No, it ain't."

"Yes, it is. Fuck you, Bowlegs." He moves towards me like he's gonna do something.

I push the chess board aside and get up. Skinny backs away.

I say, "How's about me throwing your skinny ass off the roof?"

"Googie turns off the radio and says, "Let's go."

Pidgy says, "Make your move, Johnny."

Now I can hear the thunder, and see Skinny flying through the rain like a spear and the lightening all around and him disappearing into a black cloud.

"Goddammit, Johnny, make your move. A storm is rolling in."

1951 The Red Pony

February

"All right, class, now that we've finished reading *The Red Pony*--"

Miss Ryan is giving thirty-five comatose kids the lowdown on John Steinbeck's book about some horseshit cowboys in California. The teach got this red hair and freckles and these cute Sno Balls sticking outta her chest. Soft and fluffy like the cakes. Can't keep my eyes offa them.

Last week Benjy got caught passing a note to me that said, "Would you like to see Miss R. with no clothes on?"

Pissed off, Miss Ryan sent us to the vice principal's office, and he gave us a lotta shit about keeping our peckers in our pants. Then he sent us off to detention study hall and plugged us in with some of the dumbest guys in the school. One week of talking about girls and bragging about how big our dicks were was a real education. As for our assignments, Bobby the Noodle finished them for us. We paid him off in smokes.

Back to Miss Sno Balls.

"Quiet, class. How is Jody's life like that of someone his age in New York City? Ricardo?"

"I don't have a clue, Miss."

"Nancy, what do you think?"

Nancy puts on this look like she's thinking, even props her fingers under her chin to prove it. "He's nothing like a New York kid."

"What about you, Eve?" Eve shakes her head and looks at me. Wow, that's a first.

"Daniel?"

A spitball flies past Sno Balls's head and hits the blackboard and sticks. The class giggles. She turns around and looks at it.

"I didn't see who did that, but I'm on the lookout now, and if it happens again, someone's going to be in serious trouble." She takes this ruler outta her desk and scrapes the spitball off the blackboard. "Daniel, you were going to say something?"

Daniel spent two weeks in a Kentucky barn and thinks he's a specialist.

"Well, on Grandpa's ranch it was different. All I remember was shoveling a lotta horse shit."

"Horse *manure*," says Sno Balls. She looks a little pissed.

"Sorry, I meant horse manure."

"Jerry and Matt, turn around and pay attention. Think about it, class. How is Jody's life like yours? Does he have some of the same problems? Howard?"

"Nope. He ain't nothing like us."

"He *isn't anything* like us. What about his relationship with his father? Do they get along well? Does his father understand him?"

Benjy whispers to me, "The kid's old man is a dickhead like mine."

"Benjy? Did you have something to say? Will you share it with the class?"

"No, ma'am, I didn't say nothing."

"*Anything*. Doris, what do you think?"

"Would you please repeat the question?"

"Is his father flexible? Is he willing to let Jody do things his own way?"

"No, ma'am."

"It's probably pretty common for kids to have disagreements with their fathers. Do any of you have similar problems?"

Cement faces look at her.

"Let's talk about his feeling for the pony? Remember how he felt when his first pony died? Didn't any of you ever have to put down a beloved pet?"

Still lots of cement faces.

"Ricardo, get back in your seat. Rachel, how would you describe Jody's mother?"

"I dunno. I guess she's nice."

"What does she do in the story?"

"Uh--she cooks breakfast."

"Yes. She's obviously a nurturer. That means someone who takes care of others. That's what most mothers do, isn't it?"

Sno Balls don't have a clue. Benjy's mother, who hits the bottle, is passed out most of the time, don't cook. Fact is, Sno Balls don't notice shit--like why Ricardo's scratching his head and balls all the time--and Paul's dirty shirt--and Sandra's nose running and the green loogie on her sleeve. It looks like Momma's out to lunch on all of them.

"And then we have Billy Buck, another father figure. What does the typical father do in a family? Besides being the breadwinner, I mean? Sally?"

"He picks up the Home Relief checks."

Benjy says, "He smacks the old lady around." The class snickers.

"Class, I'm serious. Isn't it his job to teach his children about life, about responsibility?"

I raise my hand. Sno Balls is shocked--never seen that before.

"John?"

"Is it like when my dad wanted to show me the ropes?"

Sno Balls claps her hands. "Exactly. What did your dad do to show you the ropes?"

"He took me to a buncha bars." The class laughs.

"Then he dragged my ass all around showing this picture I drew ."

"Say '*my rear end.*'"

"So my old man drags my *rear end* around showing my drawing with the white whale sinking the ship."

"Moby Dick?"

"Yeah."

She claps her hands again, all charged up about Moby's dick or me reading a comic book--I don't know which.

"But another time we went around to some street sellers and he helped one of them sell some of his sh-- er, stuff. He minded the cart when Tony Tomato had to go get some change."

"So he was showing you how to be a good friend?"

"Yeah, I guess so." A paper airplane sails around the room and does a kamikaze into Angelina's kinky hair.

"Matt, you need to shape up and pay attention. One more stunt like that and I'll send you to the vice principal. Now, what does Jody's father teach him?"

Daniel says, "That he'd better shape up or get his ass kicked."

"His rear end."

Julie says, "To do his chores if he wants to stay out of trouble."

"And what does Billy Buck teach Jody?"

I whisper, "That he has his nose up a horse's ass. Billy Buck's a dipshit buttinski."

In my ear Benjy says, "Living on a farm must suck. Chickens, horses--who the fuck can live--"

"John and Benjy, if you don't stop talking, I'm going to move you up here to the front row. Now, what does Billy Buck teach Jody?"

Marilyn goes, "Ooh, ooh, ooh." Her hand's waving around.

"Marilyn?"

"Billy Buck teaches him how to take care of his pony, how to be responsible. He shows him everything about it--from when it's born all the way till it's grown up."

"Very good, Marilyn." Sno Balls is excited that someone has finally figured out what she was asking for.

Benjy whispers, "What a brown-nosing little bitch."

I say, "Not much for tits--and she's got a skinny ass too." I think of Eve's gorgeous curves.

"John and Benjy, if you have something to say, say it out loud."

"Sorry," says Benjy.

Sno Balls is dishing out more of the "Tell me what I'm thinking" or "I got all the answers" questions.

By now I ain't listening. I paint me this picture of Eve and me walking through the park. We're holding hands, and I feel like a schmuck doing that, but her hand feels good, and she leads me into the woods and shows me her private place.

1951 Amnesia

March

"Say ten Hail Marys and one hundred Our Fathers."

What the fuck--a hundred Our Fathers for jerking off?

"Did you say something?"

"I didn't say nothing, Father."

"May God be with you, my son." That's the spiel to get my ass outta the booth. *Jesus Christ, a hundred. My knees won't hold up.*

Darkness. The smell of candles and incense burning. Creepy, creepy. His sad face hanging down, blood dripping--the thorns, and those eyes following me, looking at me.

I don't get it--him in pain and me in pain. *Is this shit supposed to make me better, feel better?*

I'm out in the street now. It's raining, and the city smells clean, and the streets are shining, and a girl with blue eyes and a great smile goes by me, and I can't wait to get home and jerk off.

1951 The Coal Cellar

April

Googie's down in the coal cellar, cursing and banging on the trap doors.

"What's the commotion? Who the devil is down there? Why did you call me?" says Father Callahan.

Acky says, "Googie. We're ex--horsizing him."

"Exorcizing?"

"Ever since he fell off the cab and got hisself crippled up, he's been seeing demons."

Ginzo says, "Nuh-uh, Acky. It was a truck that got him all fu-- er-- all messed up in the head. His head split open like a coconut--all the juice coming out--got me sick."

"It was a cab, " says Acky.

"A cab?" says the priest.

"He was ridin' on the suitcase rack."

"Luggage rack?"

"Listen to him--he's possessed--what's he talkin'?"

"Ah fungula, lÃšck-mi-am-arsch--bebzezat ekhtak--"

"It's Italian. And he don't speak nothing but cursive."

"Sounds like my father's Bulgarian," says the priest.

"Bebzezat ekhtak--Az moa li ti eba putkata maichina?" says Googie--and a lotta other shit we don't know, done in different kinda voices.

Acky says, "That's Wop."

"It's Bulgarian," says the father. "Really bad Bulgarian."

"Yeah, Father, every once in a while Googie gets worked up and took over. We stick him down there for curing. The possessors don't like the coal."

"You locked him up?"

"It's not us, Father--Googie told us to--'cause he forgets shit and don't know what he's doing."

"Has he done this sort of thing before?" The trap doors are doing some serious bouncing now.

Ginzo says, "Don't worry about it, Father. We've ex-horsized him in the coal cellar lotsa times. Ya gotta listen to a lotta cursing and banging, but once he gets hisself purged, you could make an altar boy outta him."

"Let us pray for him."

"Better not do that, Father."

Getting serious now, the father lifts his vestment and kneels.

"No, Father--"

He puts his hands on the door and says, "Behold, I give you the authority to trample on serpents and scorpions, and over all the power of the enemy--and nothing shall by any means hurt you--"

He goes on with a lot more shit, trying to nuke Googie to heaven. Googie don't want none of it.

"Fuck you, Father, and your whore, Mary. Lemme out."

"And Jesus rebuked the devil; and he departed out of him: and the child was cured from that very hour." Now the father's hands are shaking and the trap doors bouncing. "Open that demon gateway."

"We can't do that. The demons are still in him."

"The Lord will protect. Open the gates of hell."

"You'll hafta do that, Father--just pull at that latch," I say.

"Fuck you. Fuck Jesus. Fuck Joseph. Lemme out--there's rats running." Googie's banging hard on the wooden doors, coal dust flying. "Lemme outta this fucking hellhole."

"In the name of Jesus, be silent." His hands still on the shaking doors. "In Jesus's name, I command all demons: 'You leave at once.' I bless these doors in the name of Jesus Christ. Thank you, Lord, for your sanctification."

Hutty comes up. "Hey guys, Skinny got a Bob Feller 1948 Bowman Bubble Gum card."

"A Bob Feller?"

"Yeah, and he wants to flip for it."

I say, "Acky, you stay here, and clue us in when we get back."

"But, Johnny--"

"Hold the fort. Jesus Christ, it's a Bob Feller."

1951 Math Class

May

The bell rings. The door opens. Wham, I'm in the math class with the rest of the assholes. I go to the back row with Ginzo as usual. Eve's sittin' up a few seats in front of me, and I'm looking at her ponytail swishing around, and I wanna-- no, I don't wanna--

Mr. Tydos--we call him Tightass--is writing on the chalkboard, his pants tucked up the crack of his ass, and I can see his socks. One's blue, one's black. He must be color blind.

"Class, today we're going to review long division." The class groans.

"Oh, goody. I just love long division," says Anita Walnut. We call her Walnut 'cause of her half-shell tits. She's one of those know-it-alls who sits up front and gets hit in the head with spitballs.

Ginzo, who's next to me, says, "Is Tightass kidding? This is advanced stuff."

"Please open your books to page 40. I want you to do problems 1 through 12. Then we'll compare results."

More groaning.

"Get busy now." He reaches around and pulls his pants out of his ass crack. The trousers drop two inches and hide his socks.

We start opening books, getting out paper. Acting like we're doing something.

Tightass walks around, inspecting desks. "Lenny, get your paper out. Susan and Maria, stop talking and get to work. Ben, where's your book?"

"I forgot it."

Big mistake. Lotsa points.

"Then I'll have to take five points off your grade." He has this point system of pluses and minuses--supposed to help teach us math, I guess.

"Teacher, I need a piece of paper."

"Paper. Does anyone have a piece of paper he can lend Terry? Bob, are you working on your problems or playing with Yolanda's braids? Two points off your grade."

The class settles down and works away at the problems.

Jesus, they all have decimals, and I can't remember where to put the decimal point.

I work my way through a few of the problems, mostly just guessing what to do. Eve's head is bent over her desk. Her ponytail has fallen to the side. I can see the small golden hairs on the back of her neck.

"Done." Walnuts is sitting up straight with her arms crossed. *She's finished. Damn.*

Tightass is prowling around again. "George, you're not working. If you don't settle down, I'll have to knock off a point. Sean, do you need help? Anita, if you're finished, you can help him and earn some extra points." Sean is a pretty boy with greasy hair and all. Walnuts has this big crush on him and is always following the dum-dum around.

Walnuts, wearing her hotshit smile, moves over to Sean and bends over toward him. I think she stuffed her bra. She whispers something in his ear. Probably the answers.

Tightass moves in on me. Over my shoulder, he says, "John, you've only done five. You need to do better than that. Your grade is in serious danger."

I scrunch over, put some weight on the pencil. He moves on to the next victim. "Janet, put away that comb and do your work. You just lost one point." He goes back to the front of the room and enters a few more minus points on this big chart he has on the wall.

Janet raises her hand. "You said one point."

"You didn't put it away when I told you, so I subtracted another point." Janet mutters something I can't hear.

"Now it's blackboard time," he says. There's a rush to the pencil sharpener. Ten losers line up before I can get there.

"OK, now we'll compare. Remember, it isn't just getting the right answer. You have to show how you solved the problem. Nancy, will you put Number One on the board; George, Number Two; Yolanda Number Three." He gets to me with Number Five.

I go to the board, doing my crabwalk so Eve don't see my leg. She don't notice me for shit. Great. I do number five on the board, screwing up the numbers so nobody can read 'em.

"You'll have to redo that problem, John The numbers need to be in a format we can all understand." I erase my problem. Eve still isn't looking. I start rewriting it, improving the numbers only a little bit.

"OK, class, now let's go over these." He goes over the first four. I try to pay attention, but he goes so fast I can't follow. Then it's my turn. "Can anybody see the errors he's got here?"

Walnut's hand goes up. "He forgot to move the decimal point from the divisor over to the dividend."

Bitch.

"Right. What else? Anita, you've had a turn. How about you, Alfred?" Ginzo looks up, and then shakes his head and gives this dummy look.

"Janet?"

"When he subtracted 49 from 340, he forgot to add a 1 in the tens column."

"Good. Do you see what you did wrong, John? We've been over that enough that you should remember it."

I stand there--me, the chalk, and the eyes--and there's no exit.

1951 The Connoisseurs

July

"This place is for jerks—the line is too long, and the hot dogs suck," says Acky.

Acky's all about his gut, often risking his life climbing ledges and sneaking into buildings to scrounge up food for our merry band. Our hunter-gatherer can smell food through eight inches of concrete, so when he says the food sucks, nobody argues.

He's leading us through a forest of hotdog-hopefuls, his determined nose aimed at better eats, leaving behind Nathan's Famous Hot Dog, the bourgeois sausage. His nose sniffs through the crowd, guiding us past pots of boiling corn on the cob waiting to be bought and buttered, past pink and blue cotton candy and kids nuzzling and licking into the nothing of it. Our mouths water, our marching bellies rumble as we hoof it through the fry smells of onions and hot dogs hissing and crying in their own juices.

"What's going on?" says Googie, his crooked arm hooked on Hutty's shoulder, steering him. "You've been leading us around for half an hour. My leg hurts, and I'm getting hungry—are you lost?"

"I'm getting tired too," says Hutty.

"We'll be there soon. Just a few blocks," says Acky.

The burlap goody bag I'm carrying is getting heavy, so I hand it over to Pidgy for a while.

"When're we going to the beach?" says Ginzo. Ginzo is a swim nut. He gets his rocks off goosing the girls in the waves. His specialty is the shark trick we've brought in the bag.

"Let's stop here and have a hamburger." Pidgy points at a hamburger joint across the street.

"Nah."

"I want a hot dog."

"My mom says hot dogs are made outta leftover guts," says Ginzo. "Lots of other shit too—chicken guts—crap that fell on the floor and rolled in the sawdust—then they color it all red with paint and jam it in a thing called a 'testine--"

"That's all bullshit—I don't wanna hear that," says Acky.

"They put a lotta crap into it to hide the smell and the taste."

"It's true," Pidgy says. "Your mother must've read *The Jungle*. It's all in this guy's book about a slaughterhouse in some big city. Stuff like one guy falling into a tank of boiling lard and nobody notices. Other machines grinding up people into hamburger, sending it to Coney Island and putting it in a bun--"

I say, "Tell them the part about the rats, Pidge."

"They have these big piles of meat, and rats are running around and crapping all over it, and then the rats get sick and flop over and die. Then the whole pile of shit gets ground up and they make sausage outta it---maybe hamburger too."

"Hamburger?" says Hutty.

"That's worse," says Pidgy. "They grind 'em all up--sick animals from zoos and animal hospitals—horses, cows, sheep, pigs, chickens--all the condemned animals in the slaughterhouse—those that died in trains or trucks—anything rotten that can be ground up--"

"I ain't hungry no more," says Ginzo. "Let's go to the beach."

"What's the matter--your tummy upset?" says Googie. "Mommie's little pussy boy don't wanna eaty meaty?"

"Fuck you, Pretzel Boy."

"C'mon you guys--it's just around the corner," says Acky. "There it is."

"The Knish Kingdom?"

"Yeah, "says Acky.

"All this shit—me hopping around for hours for a fuckin' knish?"

"There's no meat in it," says Hutty.

"I ain't eating no fuckin' Jewish potato shitsack. I don't eat kosher," says Googie.

The Robbin' Hoods, "All for one and one for all"--except for Googie and his flunky Hutty.

The true hoods line up at the window and order knishes. We even get extras for the beach.

1951 The Beach Bag

July

It's a hot holiday, and a million sea worshipers on the beach have standing room only.

Sand on baloney sandwiches. Corn on the cob and faces smothered with butter. Hot dogs loaded with relish, onions, and mustard.

Now, off the boardwalk, the rumbling waves and the small shrieks of the gulls pull us through the crowd of hanging bellies and sunburned backs. The air gets wetter and heavier.

"Must be a million of 'em," says Skinny.

"Looks like there's a million in the water too."

It's the 4th of July, 1951. The temperature is 86 degrees, and the humidity is close to one hundred percent. Back in the city, the slum tenements are vacant. Here in Coney Island the sea seekers pile off the BMT Subway at Stillwell Avenue and swarm over the boardwalk--one million, three hundred thousand of them.

"What you got in the bag, Skinny?" says Hutty.

"You'll see."

"Come on—gimme a look-see."

"What's in the baggie-waggie?" says Googie.

"Up yours."

"Hey gang, there's an open spot."

By the time we get there, the horde moves in, and it's gone.

"What the shit—there's no room?" says Googie, tired now, hooked to Hutty's shoulder. "Screw the beach."

"C'mon, guys, let's find the water," says Acky.

"I'm thirsty," says Ginzo. "Let's get something to drink."

We try to sit, but there's no space—it's a wall of backs and asses.

Skinny reaches into his bag and pulls out a rubber turd. He places it carefully—visibly--on the sand, then jumps up and screams, "Oh, my God! Holy shit--it's a turd." Now Skinny has the crowd's attention. People jump, move, mostly away from Skinny, since they can't see it.

The Robbin' Hoods now have their cue and pitch in.

"Turd!"

"Look out!"

"There it is. Don't step on it!"

Some guy with real imagination says, "I can smell it."

"Someone had the shits. Lemme outta here!"

The guy with the smeller says, "Where's the turd? I can't see my feet--it's too crowded." Pushing and shoving, the mob moves away.

"Quick—spread out the towels," says Pidgy.

After we put our claim down, Acky says, "Let's go in the water–do the shark thing."

"I'm still hungry. Let's eat the knishes ," says Pidgy, reaching into the sack.

"Fuck knishes —we didn't come here for a dumb knish," says Googie. "How about a baloney sandwich? Besides, if you eat too much, you'll get the cramps." We ignore him.

Pidgy says, "Do you guys know what a baloney bowl is?"

Nobody listens to him, so he talks louder. "That's when you fry a slice and it curls up into a bowl. I do it all the time—then I fill it up with beans and cheese and lots of other stuff."

"What's he talking about?"

"Something about beans in baloney."

Pidgy continues. "There's a Finnish baloney, a German baloney, a Polish baloney called Palony—by the way, the name comes from Polonia, the old word for Poland. I think the Poles started the hot dog business hundreds of years ago."

"What did they put in 'em?" says Googie.

"You don't wanna know."

"Pass me one, Pidge." He hands me one. It's covered with sand. I try to dust it off—it just digs in.

"I guess some sand got in the bag." He hands me another.

So here we are on beach towels, eating knishes, looking for a good time.

"Let's get the fuck outta here," says Googie. "It's all farts and asses."

Skinny the Blink says, "What's the matter, Pretzel Boy—tired?"

"You want me to slap him around, Goog?" says Hutty.

"Knock it off," I say. "Let's do the jumping wallet thing."

"Yeah," says Acky.

"Let's do it," says Ginzo.

Skinny reaches into his gag bag and pushes away his supply of rubber turds, a large black shark fin, a deflated rubber truck tube and a bicycle pump. "Aha," he says, "there it is--my jumping wallet."

"Asshole," says Googie. "Every time we go to the beach you bring that same crap." Skinny pays no attention. He loves his gimmicks and gags.

"'Member the time I put shit in it, and the look on the guy's face?" says Skinny, as he lays the wallet on the sand and buries the tugging string. "He, he, he."

"Pass me one of those knishes," says Ginzo. "A pickle too."

"Whaddya think this is--the Automat? Get your own dipshit pickle," says Pidgy.

So there it is–the beckoning wallet, now on the sand, waiting. Then it happens. Sad Sack elbowing through the beach zombies, the slow sneak of his foot to the top of the wallet—then the gradual crouch to scratch his calf—the surveillance--the quick grab for fortune—and a quicker pull of the string, and Sad Sack's treasure flies out of his hand. All for a laugh.

After a few more string pulls, the zombies get wise.

"Looka the moon," says Acky, pulling down Googie's bathing suit. "Hey—look, it's got freckles."

"Asshole," says Googie, pulling up his trunks.

"Let's put on a moon party," says Ginzo.

"Yea—a moon show," says Pidgy. "Watch out, Hutty---a rhino." He points behind him. Hutty turns to look, and down go his trunks to his ankles. Pidgy hoots. Hutty, pissed, goes after him and falls, tripping on his pants. We all laugh.

White asses are now the deal; hopping and running in circles, bumping through the crowd, we drop pants and moon the beach.

"Let's go for a swim," says Ginzo.

"Lets-a go for-a swim-a," says Skinny.

"Low blow," says Hutty.

"Yeah," I say, "I'll pump up the tube for you, Googie."

"Assholes. You know I can't swim," says Googie. "I'm not going."

"Afraid of the sharky-warkies. Googie's afraid of the sharky-warkies," says Skinny.

"I'm not scared of shit."

"Yes, you are."

"Am not."

"Don't worry about it--just jam your bad leg into Sharky's mouth. He won't be able to swallow the rest of you," says Skinny.

"Ain't no sharks out there. Me and Hutty'll go out with you," says Ginzo.

"Blow up the fuckin' tube—I'm goin' out."

"Where's Skinny?"

"Heading out with the shark fin."

"Asshole."

"Hey, Goog?" Pidgy says, "did you know that a shark bit off a guy's leg at Brighton Beach last week?"

"Very funny."

"What's that?" says Ginzo, pointing out at a strange clear area of water.

That's Skinny with his dumb shark fin."

Hey, looka the people swimming away from him. He's scaring the shit outta them."

"He better watch out--the lifeguard'll get him," says Ginzo.

"Here's the tube," says Pidgy, holding it towards Googie. Undecided about what to put in first—his ass or his legs—Googie finally thinks ass and flops into it.

Ginzo and Hutty start pulling and tugging him through the swimmers and bathers. "Not that way, assholes–this way." A five-foot whitecap, and Googie tumbles out of the tube, lost. Hutty swims after him with the tube and pops him back into it, shoving him up another mountain only to have him fall back again into the bubbling fizz. Sputtering and spitting, Googie says, "Get me outta here."

"Got you," says Hutty.

"Googie," says Skinny, back now, circling around him, pushing his shark fin, "I think your tube has a leak."

"Leak? Where? What leak?"

"In the back of the tube--behind you."

"I can't see—Hutty, is there a leak?"

"Nah, he's bullshitting you. It's only fart bubbles."

It was later folklore on the block that Skinny's rubber shark fin started the great Fourth of July Big Fish Story that terrorized Coney Island and did more damage that day than all the sunburn.

1951 The Parachute

July

"You're chicken shit—wuk, wuk, wuk," says Skinny the Blink.

"No, I'm not."

"Yes, you are."

"Am not."

"Are too."

I look up at all two hundred and sixty-two feet of the Parachute.

Maybe it'll get stuck up there at the top. Maybe the chute won't open. What if it breaks loose and goes out to sea? I don't wanna do this. I don't feel good.

Then Hutty, Ginzo, and Pidgy pitch in.

"Don't let him call you chicken."

"Bo's no chickenshit."

Pidgy says, "Leave him alone—quit pushing. He's going to do it."

"Nobody's pushing," says Skinny, "I'll even go up with him and hold his pansy-assed hand."

Googie pops in with a dare, a double dare, and a triple dare.

Acky says, "My brother's not chicken. Kick his ass, Johnny."

What else can I do? This is war, and my reputation's at stake. Skinny, like Acky, apparently has no fear of heights. Me? I'm scared shitless.

The 262-foot tall Parachute tower has twelve chutes, each thirty-two feet in diameter when open. Twelve steel umbrellas radiate from the top of the central structure. The chutes are suspended above canvas seats tied to cables that run from the ground up to the umbrellas. Each seat carries two passengers who are strapped in and hoisted up. When a parachute hits the top, it stretches out and opens as it drops--violently at first, then gradually slower, billowing out for the trip down.

A parachute with two girls lands right in front of us with a whump. Their faces are white.

"Step down, girlies—be careful. Let me help you there, Blondie," says the grease-spotted attendant, his filthy hands reaching towards her. Blondie cringes away. He goes for the other. "Ugh," she says, "please let me do it myself," holding her hands up and away.

"I'll never do that again—it was terrible," says Blondie.

"It was like being pushed off a cliff--I thought it would never slow down," says the other.

"Let's move along, girlies–hey you, the skinny kid—you first. Put your ass down there." The grease bum moves towards Skinny and points at the canvas sack the two girls got out of.

"Keep your greasy hands offa me--I can do it myself."

"OK---hey, you with the bowlegs—you're next."

I want to make a nasty comment but think it's better to keep quiet. I eye the seat suspiciously. It looks like it's going to split in half. "What is this—can't we wait for the next one?"

"Don't worry about the seat, Bowlegs—this is one of the good ones," says Grease Bum. "If it comes apart, just grab ahold of the cable and slide on down. Haw, haw."

"Come on, Bo," says Skinny, "You're not punking out?"

By now all the guys are laughing at me, and fuckin' Skinny is the hero. That's a first.

"You look a little green around the gills, kid. Don't you like heights? Haw, haw," says Grease Bum. I wonder if he's part of the show.

"I'm not scared of nothing."

Grease Bum says, "You guys ready?" He waits a long time, grinning. Waiting for me to chicken out. I put my ass into the bucket with Skinny, who's having a ball laughing at me. I grab on to the straps–real tight–like they're going to save me.

Bored now, Grease Bum looks around for others to torment. He sees no one else; then he does a wide, rotten-teeth smile and pulls the lever. "Upsy-daisy—have fun, kiddies." The chute goes up with a jerk, and I almost shit my pants. I can hear everyone laughing at me.

"Isn't this great?" says Skinny. Our legs dangling, canvas seat squeaking, me looking between my feet, ground dropping below. Fifty feet. Now moving faster. Steeplechase Park below is shrinking. One hundred feet. The Robbin' Hoods are smaller—waving—still laughing at me--safe on the ground. Goodbye, gang. Hello, death.

"Isn't it getting a little windy up here?" says Skinny. The chair is blowing around a bit.

I don't say nothing, just waiting for this thing to hit the top and bring me down. We're halfway up. I see a guy and girl on another chute. The girl grabs her boyfriend--scared shit—her legs are kicking, looking for ground. Then she screams like the cat Googie threw off the roof.

Skinny, looking at her, says, "I don't feel good. I wanna go down."

I say, "Jump. Here, I'll loosen the belt for you." I fumble around with the safety system, trying to pass my fear over to him.

"Stop fuckin' around—this is serious." Skinny's body gets stiff; his face is white.

I'm looking at my shoe. It's coming loose. Can a sneaker kill someone?

One hundred and eighty feet. People's faces shrivel into dots, and the dots blend into a black mass that stretches out along the boardwalk and beach. Two hundred and ten. Strangely, the fear oozes out of me as I listen to the joysounds around Steeplechase Park's ten-cent kingdom. The Tilt-a-Whirl dipping and spinning, keeping riders in a constantly shifting state of disequilibrium. The kick of the two Dutch shoes, their long legs swinging in opposite directions, gradually higher and higher till they're upside down, frozen at the top—the riders upside down, screaming, waiting for the fall. Then the roller coaster's slow, creepy click-click-click to the top—the hover—the pause–and then the drop and the roar into breathlessness.

Two guys in another chute are waving at us, laughing, pointing at the Wonder Wheel. I wave back. Up. Up. See Bo go up.

"Bo—I'm scared."

Skinny grabs my leg. I shove his hand away. This frightens him even more. Now, crushing the straps, his knuckles are white. He begins to pray, "Our father who art in heaven, hollow be thy virgin, thy kingdom come, full of grace--"

Fear is a funny thing. I laugh and enjoy the trip down.

1951 The Freak Show

July

"Hur-ry, hur-ry, hur-ry, step this way for the strangest sights on Coney Island. See freaks from all four corners of the world—for two nickels–one dime--the tenth part of a dollar. We've got the show if you've got the dime.

"See the Pin-Headed Family; watch the Turtle Man work with no arms. Hur-ry, hur-ry, hur-ry." The carny barker between two jiggling belly dancers points at a banner with his cane. "For those who want more, see the three-breasted bearded lady."

"Hur-ry, hur-ry, hur-ry." Then he points at the belly dancers with their undulating arms and pumping bellies, inviting us. "See more like these. There are skinny ones--there are fat ones--they're all inside. Get the whole show now for one thin dime. Hur-ry, hur-ry, hur-ry, the door is closing."

"Three tits—imagine that," says Googie as he props his hand on Hutty for balance, hobbling and hopping beside him.

"Look-a, look-a, look-a." The barker points at the huge banner full of images of freaks. "See the Elephant Woman from the darkest part of Africa. Talk to Jack Dracula, the Tattooed Beast of Transylvania. See, the Seal Boy eat live fish and build a bench with his little flippers. Listen to Zoho our talking chimp. He'll tell your fortune. Hur-ry, hur-ry, hur-ry, the curtain is going up—two nickels—one thin dime."

"Wow, a talking chimp," says Skinny. "I'm going."

"Me too," says Googie. "I wanna see the three tits."

"Me too," says Hutty.

Acky, me, and Pidgy agree and follow.

This is a first--the Robbin' Hoods all agree on something without a meeting.

* * * * * * *

"That sucked," says Googie, "She had three tits the size of walnuts—not like the picture."

Skinny the Blink says, "That Dracula guy was just a bull-shitter with tattoos--we got took."

Acky says, "The talking chimp was fake—just a lotta grunts and arm waving."

"That was sign language—a sort of talk," says Pidgy.

"Bullshit," says Googie. "The monkey was just waving his arms around to get them to throw food at him."

"It's not a monkey—it's a chimpanzee," says Pidgy, "a member of the ape family--supposed to be very smart."

"Smarter than you, you asshole—because you fell for it."

"Actually, the ape is known to have a brain bigger than yours."

"Your mother fucked with a monkey."

"That has some truth in it . Once we swung out of trees and stood on two feet, our brains developed and we moved rapidly from ape to man. So, as you said, our mothers 'fucked with monkeys.'"

"Where did you get that, outta a comic book?"

"Problem is, some of us stayed up on the trees and never came down. Throwbacks hanging around in trees, throwing stones and coconuts--everybody's an enemy."

"Fuck you--my mom never slept with no monkey--them's niggers you're talking about."

"That's an illogical jump."

"A what?"

"Your mother being jumped by a monkey."

Googie always has a comeback, but this time he stands there like someone hit him with a brick.

"The Seal Boy was a bunch of bullshit," says Hutty, coming to Googie's rescue.

Pidgy says, "Wasn't it amazing how a guy with no arms could build furniture with those little tiny flippers?"

Googie says, "Just what the world needs—a handyman with no arms—a freaky fuckin' seal man making benches with his flippers."

Hutty, his crutch, says, "Right on, Googie."

"Hey, Googie," says Skinny, "I got an idea."

Googie says, "That'll be a first."

"You apply for a job at the freak show."

Everybody laughs.

"You tell the carny guy you just hopped outta the oven. You say you're Pretzel Boy, the latest thing in half-baked freaks."

"Ouch."

"Low blow."

"Nasty."

Googie has three choices. One, look for a comeback. Two, get Hutty to kick Skinny's ass. Three, just shut up. No, I take that back--Googie isn't into shutting up.

"Is your pants dry yet?"

"My pants?" says Skinny.

"Yeah—your pants—the ones you pissed in when you were up there in the parachute." He points at Skinny's crotch.

Lots of laughing from the gang.

"I never pissed in my pants—that's a lie."

"Look—there's the evidence." He points again, There's nothing there, but we all start to see it--maybe because we want to.

Skinny, trying to get off the subject of his pants, says, "OK, so you don't like Pretzel Boy. How about you and Hutty teaming up as the Leech and--and--I'll think of something for Hutty the Hump."

"Why--I'll kick your punky ass." Hutty charges towards Skinny, and Googie almost falls.

I say, "Let's lay offa the mitts." Hutty backs off. He's always been a little scared of me.

Googie latches onto his ride again and straightens himself out. It takes a while. His long red hair is a mess. He whips out his comb. Most of us laugh; we know he's stalling for time when he does the comb bit. He don't say nothing more—just keeps staring at Skinny's pants.

"I'm no punk—and I never pissed in my pants."

We all keep looking at his crotch and the stain grows— even though it isn't there.

1951 The Lead Penny

July

Pidgy scrapes and rubs the lead penny on the cement walkway, scratching his knuckles in the process. By now Lincoln's zinc face is gone, and Pidge is working on the rolling edge, scraping it into the dime size we need.

"How'd we ever let the others go on without us? One of them woulda had a dime for the subway."

"Dammit, my fingers are getting sore. Maybe we should check out the boardwalk and see if any dimes fell through the cracks."

"You've almost got it. Keep scraping."

"This isn't going to work—it'll make the alarm go off."

"There's no alarm. Quit imagining things."

"This sucks."

Stuck in Coney Island with one dime between us, Pidgy and I take turns scraping away at his lead penny, shooting for big money and carfare home.

1951 Waiting for the Dentist

August

The long hallway smells like carbolic acid. I'm sitting on a bench with a lot of raggedy-assed kids and their moms. There's a few old farts reading newspapers or dozing off. My little brothers are skidding back and forth on the waxed hallway, bumping into whoever gets in their way.

"Richard, Charley, quit that. You're bothering people," says Ma. They don't listen and continue with their roller derby.

Most of us have been here since early morning, waiting for them to do something. The kid on the bench across from me has this ice pack on his jaw and keeps rocking his head back and forth. His mom has her arm on his shoulder, comforting him.

My ma, as always, chewed up by the system, says, "There's just a few more people in front of us, and they should be getting to us pretty soon." She grabs my hand; I pull it away. "Is it still hurting?"

"Nah, Ma. I don't feel a thing."

I hear some grunting, groaning and thumping coming from the room behind me. With my back against the wall, I feel something banging--probably his feet.

Ice Jaw says to me, "Can't they give him something?" He looks concerned. "Did they give you anything?"

"Nah, that's just for the sissies on Park Avenue."

"No shit," says Ice Jaw.

There's more banging behind me. I turn around and glance at the wall, "I don't know how the guy behind me got his legs free; they usually jump on your knees and hold 'em down."

Ice Jaw is really scared now. His eyes look bigger.

"Then this guy climbs into your mouth with these huge pliers and gives it a twist or two. Once he hears it crack--kind of a crunching sound--he jerks it one way, then another; then it explodes and comes out--roots and all–blood gushing everywhere."

"Stop that kind of talk," says my mother. Ice Jaw scrunches up his crotch; is he going to piss in his pants?

Five minutes later the kid with the banging feet comes out of the room, holding his jaw and crying. All of us look up at him and feel sorry for ourselves and what's coming.

1951 Movies

August

"I'm sick of movies---all you wanna do is see movies." Pidgy's a pain in the ass—whenever I wanna do something, he has a better idea.

"Yeah, yeah. You do the books, and I do the movies."

"My feet are sore."

"Forget the feet."

"But they hurt."

"Put more cardboard in your shoes."

"I use linoleum."

This goes on until we arrive at 42nd Street between Seventh and Eighth Avenue. "Look—the Lyric has Comedy Day," I say.

"I want a cowboy movie."

"But 'Looney Tunes'—The Three Stooges—Abbott and Costello?"

"Let's go to the Apollo. Look, they're playing 'Along Came Jones' with Gary Cooper." He gets sidetracked again. "Hey, let's get a hamburger."

"Too expensive."

"Fifteen cents?"

"I don't have fifteen cents," I say.

"There's a place selling them for a dime." He points next door.

"I'm not hungry. Besides they're all bun."

"I'm not into any comedies." Pissed off. He stands there, right in the middle of the zombies.

"Get outta the way, Punk," says a walking dead.

Pidgy makes like a chicken, hands on hips, flapping his elbows. "Wuk, wuk, wuk. Fuck you, and your momma too."

"Asshole," says the zombie. His numb face fades into the crowd.

42nd Street between Seventh and Eighth Avenues in the early 1950s was packed with movie houses on both sides. For me it was a five-block walk into a larger world of dreams. I was still reading comic books, and TV was an experiment for the rich. There was only 42nd Street and its movie houses. Cowboys and Indians, boring romances, swashbuckling sea battles, the Bowery Boys, steel-jawed soldiers jumping into fox holes, Tweety Bird and Sylvester. I fell in love with Hollywood, but 42nd St. was its address.

"Too bad Acky ain't here."

I'm screwing around with the can opener and can't get it into the door's crack.

"Come on, come on, someone's coming. Jesus Christ, hurry up." Sometimes Pidgy is a little chickenshit.

"There—I got it," I say, as I pry the fire door open.

"Let's go to the balcony. Plenty of seats."

"There's the Coke machine—I'll get us some drinks." After looking around, I reach into the machine and yank down a cup. Soda pours into it. I do it again for Pidgy. I do it two more times to get empty cups, letting the soda go down the drain.

"Let's get some popcorn."

"It's your turn."

"Nuh-uh, it's your turn. Besides the girl over there is watching."

The girl behind the candy counter is about sixteen and loaded with pimples. We sit a while across from her and watch.

Walking over, I say, "Hey, girlie, I'm looking for a job. They doing any hiring?" Pidgy moves next to the popcorn.

Pimple Face looks at me and puts me in the maggot department. "We don't hire children." Of course she don't do any hiring–she just pops popcorn and peddles candy. Pidgy moves in a little closer to where he has to be. Pimple Face puts the eye on him.

I say, "Something popped."

"Popped?" she says. "What popped?"

"One of those." I point at her face.

"Oh, my god." She rushes to her handbag and pulls out a mirror. "Where is it? I don't see it."

Pidgy moves in on the popcorn and starts filling the cups.

"I don't see a thing."

I say, "The one right next to the blackhead." I'm in close now, pointing where she ain't looking and blocking her view.

"Blackhead—what blackhead?" Now she's really working the mirror.

Pidgy—the cups running over with popcorn--goes for a few candy bars.

She looks like she's going to cry. I'm starting to feel sorry for her. She's kinda pretty under the pimples. Besides I have the same problem, and it ain't funny.

"I can't stand this job," she says. "Too many people--" She's putting some crap on her face to hide the craters and mountains. She starts to cry, and I feel like shit.

Up on the balcony we find seats on the front row and-- guess what? Hutty and Googie are there. We don't sit near them cause they're a pain in the ass, but that don't bother them; they love being a pain in the ass. So they move through the crowd, Googie falling on people as he hops and limps through, then sitting down right next to me. Like I said, a pain in the ass.

Just about now the Road Runner and the Coyote are doing their usual on the screen. The coyote—who's supposed to be smart--pushes a boulder off a cliff to get the Road Runner; then he runs down to see a close-up of the action.

Googie says, "I hate the Road Runner."

I say, "Good, so you hate the Road Runner."

"Me too," says Hutty.

"Knock it off, you guys," says a zombie behind us.

"Fuck you, Jersey." Hutty throws some popcorn at the guy. He hates guys from Brooklyn, but sometimes he gets things mixed. Probably thinks Jersey is in Brooklyn.

The guy in the back leans over to us. He's big. But when we all turn and smile, he decides we have the poundage. Hutty starts tossing popcorn over the balcony. "Look, it's snowing," he says.

I say, "Quit that shit."

Pidgy says, "C'mon, guys. Knock it off."

Googie says, "Yeah, it's snowing." He begins tossing popcorn with Hutty. The zombies below wake up. Someone turns on a flashlight.

I say, "Duck, you assholes. They'll throw us out." The flashlight goes out and we hear the zombies moving around in the dark.

Movietone news comes up and gives us the lowdown on the world in 1951.

> *--in spite of Soviet Russia's attempt to wreck the San Francisco Japanese Peace Treaty Conference attended by fifty two nations...moves to a successful conclusion...final hours highlighted by John Dulles exposing Soviet plans to make the Sea of Japan a Russian lake...the determined opposition of the free nations of the world...bring to the North Koreans the truth about their communist oppressors--*

"What is this shit? When are the cartoons coming up?" says Googie.

"Quiet, you Commie," says a zombie somewhere in back.

"It's that crippled fuck up front," says another.

* * * * * * *

Outside, small rain falling, and the street's shining. I can see the clouds in the cement.

"I like Abbott and Costello," says Pidgy.

"Me, I'm for the Three Stooges," says Hutty.

"My pick is the Road Runner and the Coyote," I say.

"Fuck you guys and comedies," says Googie, lurching a bit, hanging like a leech, his arm on Hutty's shoulder, steering him back to the block.

"How's about we get some hot dogs?" says Pidgy.

We all look at him, at each other, waiting for someone to come up with the cash. Nothing.

1951 Chess

August

We're on the roof again, and the sun's going down. The windows on the skyscrapers are catching the red, and shadows are moving from building to building. There's a ship coming in to dock, and I can hear tugboats talking to it. Ravel's "Bolero" is playing on the Victrola.

Pidgy moves his queen, his skinny fingers shoving my king in a corner. I'm two moves ahead, but Pidgy's three. I'm going down.

Pidgy says, "Did you hear that shit last night?"

"Yeah, woke us up."

"Us too."

"Sounded like a bag of garbage."

"More like a potato sack."

"More like a carrot sack."

"How about a crate of eggs?"

"When I got up in the morning, it was gross--his head was squashed--blood all over the place."

"Turned my stomach."

"You see where his wooden leg was? He musta tossed it off first--like twenty feet away."

I flip my dincher off into the air shaft and watch it spin into the garbage below.

What was he thinking? His leg flipping through the air and him following. Him laying there dead for hours--garbage all around him and the cops picking up his leg. And Andy

Corcus mopping up his blood. And Andy stuttering and mumbling some fucked-up prayer for a guy with no leg who's going to the dump.

I say, "Who gives two fucks about a twirling bum with a bad leg? Lotsa people have bad legs."

"I kinda felt sorry for him, poor bastard. Maybe he had kids."

"He was just a bum."

I get tired of waiting for Pidge to make his next move, so I go over to the ledge and look down at the street.

Old Lady Piper's leaning outta her window, policing the street, her big nose looking this way and that.

John the Iceman, his wide ass chugging--an ice block balanced on his shoulder--the tongs and burlap sack to keep control--is heading towards our building–up maybe six flights–ice for iceboxes--for those who got the cash.

Some spic music is coming from a window under us and bouncing around off the buildings.

"Checkmate," Pidgy says.

"Yeah, OK."

Pidgy gathers the chess pieces and puts them in the box. "What're we gonna do tomorrow?"

"More chess? So you can beat the shit outta me again?"

Part 3: The Pressure Cooker

1951 Pimples

September

Me and Popeye, one of the big guys, are having a smoke under the street light--the bulb is on and off. Down the block someone knocks over a garbage can, and I wait for the voices. Nothing. Then more nothing. Then-- "Take your whoring bitch and get out." A door slams. More nothing. The streetlight goes out.

Ginzo rolls the dice into the darkness. I can hear them bouncing. "Seven," he says, pointing at them as the light pops and sputters on.

"What the fuck--you picked 'em up before I could see," says Googie.

"I'll do it again." Ginzo blows on them three times and gives them a good rattle to his ears. He's waiting for the light to short out again. I hear the roll, but I don't see the dice-- then I do--and Ginzo says, "Seven."

"Fuck you," says Googie, "you cheating prick--you switched them." Googie picks up his money. Ginzo laughs.

Pidgy and Acky come up. "What's with the light?" says Acky.

"Where you been?" I ask.

"Looking for spinach," says Acky. Pidgy laughs. I mentioned spinach to Popeye one time, and he slapped the shit outta me.

Popeye lets that one slide--he's fixed on my nose.

"Use Ivory soap every day and it'll clear up. Stop jerking off--that's probably the main cause."

"Really?" I laugh to myself. He must've done a lotta jerking. His face is full of huge craters and washes from spanking the love button.

"It's got something to do with glands," says Pidgy.

"What glands?"

"Who the fuck knows? Glands are glands," says Popeye.

"I just studied glands. There's a lot of them--pituitary, thyroid--"

"Which one of them controls the face?" I say.

"Why?" says Acky.

"The face is important," says Pidgy. "It's the first thing a guy looks at in a girl. It gets him right in the balls. By the way, balls are a gland. Tits and asses have to stand in line."

"I don't know about that--the first thing I look at is the tits."

"They say it's in the blood--some guys like heart-shaped faces, others like oval. Big lips, a curved-up nose--Irish guys like that."

"What about squareheads? Do Swedes like square heads?" That one slipped out--better watch myself.

"I'm Norwegian. Back to the pimples. They got this shit called Clearasil, and it don't work to get rid of 'em--just hides 'em."

The prick is on my nose again. Clearasil. That's what I got on my volcano. Looks like it didn't work. What if it's still there this weekend?

"After a while the shit cracks from the sweat." He's looking right at it.

The streetlight keeps flashing, spotlighting my nose.

Bad enough that I got this crooked leg and have to scuttle around the girls like a bottom-sucking crab. Maybe Eve will go blind and fall in love with my voice--maybe this fucking Vesuvius on my nose will have a miracle and explode.

1951 Retribution

September

"I had this dream about Wonder Woman and pole vaulted outta my bed."

"Make a move--stop daydreaming."

"You know the saying that you get hair on your palm--"

"I heard the story. Make your move." This time Pidgy points to the chessboard to get me moving.

"Look," I hold out my hand and point at my palm. "Is there a little hair there?"

"For chrissakes, move."

Skinny the Blink comes up to us on the roof. "Whazzup?" He has a paper bag in his hand.

I say, "Checkers."

"That ain't checkers--that's chess."

Pidgy says, "We didn't have checker pieces so we used chess pieces."

"Huh?"

"We're playing checkers with chess."

"It's a whole new game."

"We move in any way we want."

Skinny says, "You guys are fucking with me."

"What's in the bag?"

"Shit."

"Shit?"

"What for?"

"That prick watchman next door."

The roof of 525 is an ammo supply dump for Skinny's deadly missiles--cat shit, dog shit, and occasional human shit. The Blink can't see too well, but he always finds his target. Only the drunk and ignorant wander into his bombing range.

"What did he do?"

"Kicked me in the ass." He spots a dried turd and scoops it up with a kid's sand shovel.

"For what?"

"I was getting us some cream puffs, and this foot comes outta nowhere." He jiggles and hefts his bag, then takes a smell. "Perfect."

"When?"

"Tonight. Wanna watch?"

"No, thanks."

1951 God

September

Our father which art in heaven, hallowed be thy name. Thy kingdom come; thy will be done. Your blood, your spikes, your dripping thorns, your twisted body nailed to my memory follows me.

God, was I afraid of you.

When I was twelve my old man thought it would be a great idea for me to go to Sacred Heart of Jesus Catholic School and have God scare the fear of hell into me--not my brothers, just me. I guess I was my old man's test pilot.

The old man was a good Catholic, always blessing himself when passing the church, lighting candles whenever the welfare check was late, and having all of his sons baptized. As evidence of our baptism, he had a group photo taken of Acky and me in our sailor suits with our parents and godparents, all there, fixed in time and black-and-white. No smiles, lots of suits and dresses, a solemn occasion.

Once I started class at Sacred Heart of Jesus, black swallowed me--black robes, dark corners, and the mystery of sin. The only thing positive about this new situation was the darkness that gave me a sanctuary for my pimples.

Sacred Heart was in Hell's Kitchen just a few blocks from our flat on 47th Street. Classes went from grades 1 through 8. The boys were on one side and girls on the other. The courtyard had a line in the middle we never crossed.

It had been a girls' school, but in 1924 the boys' division was started and staffed by the Christian Brothers of

Ireland, who had "a strong reputation for discipline." Some have called it physical and sexual abuse. In the 1950's, when I was there, there were 1200 students, mostly of Irish-American heritage. The diocese apparently thought that, since the neighborhood was crawling with Irish drunks fist-fighting in the streets, in the bars, and in their homes, the only way to discipline us and point us to the ways of God was to call in their muscle—the Wise Guys from Ireland.

In 2011 The Christian Brothers Institute, a New York holding company declared bankruptcy after ten-plus years of lawsuits that alleged CBI profited while its Christian Brothers members sexually abused children. My story is not about sexual abuse—if it was there, it was in a darkness deeper than mine.

"Hold out your hand and keep it there!" Swoosh goes the rubber strap as I jerk my hand back again and again, trying to avoid the unavoidable.

I've missed two Sunday masses, and Brother McMichael is giving me "a small sample of what Jesus went through."

"I told you not to pull back." Brother McMichael grabs my wrist and smacks away. *What is this shit? Jesus is supposed to be kind and loving—and this motherfucking prick is whaling away on my hand and giving me a sample of his love?*

"Uhhh," I try not to cry out, my hand red, throbbing, and me tugging, him tugging. Whack. Whack. The pain spreads out, my fingers numb.

"What is the chief end of man?" His face is red, veins bubbling on his temples.

Whack. His hand-carved rubber strap hisses like a snake when he swings.

I say, "To glorify God and--and--and enjoy him forever."

He asks, "What rule hath God given to direct us how we may glorify and enjoy Him?" He stares closely at my hand as though there are demons dancing on it.

I'm rattled but have no fucking tears for him. *Up yours— you fucking sonofabitch.*

"The word of God--which is in the—uh, which is contained in the scriptures of the--uh, of the Old and New Testaments--is the only rule to direct us-- uh, to direct us-- to direct us how we may—how we may glorify and enjoy Him." When is this shit going to end?

Satisfied that he's knocked the devil out of me, he puts his homemade strap in his desk and says, "Study harder next time. Go sit, and don't miss Sunday mass again." I sit; my hand throbs and is starting to swell. I think I'm going to piss in my pants. That cocksucker--some day I'll get him in an alley and stuff his balls up his ass.

On the way home looking at my disaster of a right hand, I wonder whether I'll still be able to jerk off with it, and whether it'd be as much fun using the left. When I get home I'll find out.

1951 The Altar Boys

October

Yeah, I know it sounds weird. Me an altar boy. I'll give credit to my old man for that.

We're at Sacred Heart. Don't know why they call it that. Brother McGeeney is giving twelve of us a lecture on what it takes.

"Throughout the mass, genuflect whenever approaching, leaving, or walking across the front of the altar."

The other guys in the class are waiting for my signal.

Walking back and forth, McGeeney grabs his cassock and swirls it around like a bullfighter. He's airing out something, his balls or maybe an early morning fart.

He goes on, "When all get to the front of the altar and genuflect, the altar boy on the right takes the priest's biretta from him and puts it aside."

Ginzo, next to me says, "What's a berrieta?"

I say, "It's a gun, stupid. Don't you know anything?"

"What they want a gun in a church for?"

"Protection. In case God went to Coney Island."

McGeeney moves in on Ginzo and me and gives us the evil eye.

"You altar boys kneel on the floor on each side of the priest--"

I put my hand up.

"What is it?"

"I got bad knees. Do I get more points if it hurts when I kneel?" The back row snickers.

He don't pay me no attention and goes on. "Make the sign of the cross whenever the priest does. Bow toward the priest while saying 'Misereatur tibi.' Bow down while reciting the Confiteor, and strike the breast three times when saying 'Mea culpa.'"

Then he goes on with more of the gymnastics. "Repeat after me, 'Ad Déum qui laetíficat juventútem méam.'"

Some ass-kisser waves his hand and says, "Ooh, ooh, ooh."

"Yes, Frederick? What is it?"

Frederick says, "Adam quee terrific at juvenile, ma'am."

"Not even close," says the brother.

I say, "What's it all mean, Brother?'

"You don't need to know. Just memorize it and say it at the right time."

Asshole.

"Now all repeat after me one more time--" He's not looking now. I load my straw and hit the blackboard with a spitball. Splat.

"Who did that?" He goes for his desk, gets out the strap. He paces back and forth, slapping his strap in his hand. His cassock is swirling. "Where are you, you little devil?"

A voice in the back whispers, "I confess, Brother." A hand goes up. "I confess." Another hand goes up. "I confess." Waving arms pop up all over. "I confess." "We confess." Some wiseass showoff says, "Confiteor."

I never made it to altar boy. Flunked out the first month.

1952 Upstate

June

Acky says, "No way."

"It'll be great. Free food and a place to flop. Woods, lakes, and stuff like that."

Acky's never been off the block except for Central Park and Coney Island--and I think maybe for the first time he's a bit scared--and that's saying a lot 'cause Acky ain't never scared.

"Tell you what. I'll give you the fishing pole."

I got me this fishing pole Skinny the Blink stole and left for me to watch.

"Shove your pole. I don't want it."

"You could bring it when we go to Bear Mountains. Their house is near a lake. Lots of big fish."

Acky's a sucker for fishing. Maybe I can get him to bite.

"What's with the Bear Mountain thing--they got bears?"

"That's just the name of the mountains."

"What happened to the bears?"

"They got killed."

"What for?"

"Dunno--people ate them or something."

"People don't eat bears. The bears eat people."

"Forget about the bears."

Sometimes Acky's like Pidgy--once he gets something in his head, he won't stop.

"Who are these people we're supposed to stay with?"

"The Griffins. They got this big house. And they set up this deal with the YMCA to stick guys like us in their house for two weeks."

"Do we hafta pray?"

"Nah, where'd you get that idea?"

"What's in it for us?"

"So's we can act like rich guys and get an experience."

"What's that?"

"Experience?"

He nods.

"Like being a rich guy for a while. You know--like the book where this raggedy-assed kid becomes a prince."

"Nah, I ain't read that." Acky never reads.

"The Griffins got two kids--one's about our age--and we can live with them for free."

"Yeah, I know--Ozzie and Harriet and their kids. We can hunt bears with 'em."

This is gonna cost me.

"Look, I'll tell you what. I'll toss in the tackle box."

"Tackle box? You got the tackle box?"

"Yeah, Skinny left it with me. But screw him, I'll give it to you."

"What about the Robbin' Hoods? What are they gonna say about us fucking around with the bears?"

Acky's a tough nut. "Never try to con a con." That's what Pops says.

"I'll get Pidgy to lend you his bike for a week--and that's it."

"Deal."

The Griffins

There's six of us. We're all sitting at this table, and we're just getting ready to eat, and there's a white tablecloth and cloth napkins. Just like the movies.

It's not Thanksgiving or anything like that--just Sunday dinner--I've never seen such a spread. There's this big roast, and a dish of gravy, and a huge bowl of mashed potatoes, and some peas. They're bright green, not like the ones we get out of a can.

Mr. Griffin--I'll call him Mr. Ozzie 'cause Acky was right--says, "I believe it's my turn to say grace. Unless-- Johnny, Axel, would you like to take a turn?"

Acky says, "No way."

"No thanks," I say.

"Well, maybe next time," he says. "All right then. For what we are about to receive, may the Lord make us truly thankful. Amen."

We've been here a week. They gave me and Acky a room of our own--with two real beds, and they always eat meals together--imagine that. Their daughter Margie is sixteen and has some beautiful tits, but I don't think she likes us 'cause she treats us like shitbags. She's always fiddling with her hair or her makeup or going out with dipshits. Roger, their son, is Acky's age and is a bit brainy. He don't get along with Acky--I think Acky's afraid of how smart he is and wants to smack his fat ass around. I kinda like him. He's a good bullshitter for a rich kid.

Back to the meal. I'm glad Mr. Ozzie keeps the prayer short. Mrs. Harriet always goes on and on about the Lord's blessing and a lotta shit about all the great things they got and how Jesus died to make things better for her-- maybe so's she can get more shit.

This is a great dinner. I eat everything on my plate. Mrs. Harriet offers me more, and I take all she throws at me.

"What's this?" says Acky.

I give him the elbow and whisper, "Those are peas, stupid. Eat them and shut up."

"I don't like peas."

"Give 'em to me, then."

"I thought we could go to the mountains tomorrow," says Mrs. Harriet. "I'll pack a picnic lunch."

Yay," says Roger. "I like that."

"I think Johnny and Acky will like it too," says Mr. Ozzie. "Too bad I have to work and can't go with you."

Roger says, "Can we bring liverwurst sandwiches for Johnny?"

I say, "With mustard and butter and maybe on a roll--the kind with seeds?" I'm pushing it, but what the hell.

Acky says, "Hey, what about me? I like liverwurst too."

Well, whoop-de-doo, Acky likes liverwurst too. Why can't the asshole be nice?

The Catskill Mountains

The Park Ranger's giving us his spiel about the Park. He's all spiffed up like Smokey the Bear, hat and all--you'd think he was some kinda general. He just gave us the lowdown on a lotta shit about not burning the woods down. Now he's sliding into the big picture.

"New York's Catskill Mountains include one of the largest and most complex natural areas in the East, on a par with the West's Yellowstone National Park. Round, forested mountains; narrow, winding valleys; rushing streams and rivers are features that attract many to the 600,000 acres of the Catskill Park."

Acky says, "When do we get the liverwurst sandwiches?"

"One of the best kept New York State secrets is Bear Spring Mountain Campground, well-known for its excellent hunting and fishing, as well as its facilities for campers with horses."

Acky says "Will we be able to get a bear burger there?" *Asshole.*

Margie gives Acky the evil eye. She sure has some nice tits. Love to get my hands under that sweater.

"Let's go, Mother. We've heard all this before," says Roger.

Hiking the Trail

She called me an urchin--what's that?

"Acky says to me, "What's with this hiking shit?" He's carrying his fishing pole and tackle box. "Why don't you carry this for a while?"

"You're the fisherman."

"You're the one who wanted to be Davy Crockett."

I say, "Keep your voice down."

"When do we eat?"

Mrs. Harriet says, "Another mile and we'll be at the lake."

"Another mile?"

"Look around you," she says. "Look at these majestic trees, the delicate ferns, the ivy, the birds, the squirrels. This is Nature's bounty, given to us by God for our use and pleasure. How can you see all this and not feel his presence and his abundant love? I think it's a manifestation of the Holy Spirit."

She goes on about the woods and how God laid it all out for us and how all the plants and the dumb animals are there for us to use and how we just need to listen to God to know what to do.

A squirrel runs across the path. I watch it go up and around a tree and look at me from the other side.

Margie has these long legs and moves fast, her tits rolling up and down. Something's rising in my pants. I try not to look at her. Can't do that. So I slide back behind her and watch the pine trees whiz by with the sun peeking through.

I get a hard-on anyway.

The Lake

Finally we're at the lake. It's a bright blue with these huge trees around it. The picnic ground's right in front.

"Uh-oh," says Roger. "Look." He points at a sign that says NO FISHING.

"No fishing?" says Acky. "What good is a lake with no fishing? The hell with the sign. I'm gonna do it anyway."

"You can't," says Roger. "My mom would have to pay a big fine."

"Shit." Acky throws the pole on the ground. I pick it up. *Asshole.*

Mrs. Harriet says, "Roger, why don't you take Johnny and Acky down to the lake and back while Margie and I get the lunch ready." She takes a tablecloth out of her basket. Would you believe it? A tablecloth? For a picnic?

Roger says, "See that fern?"

Acky says, "What?"

"It's a *Thelypteris noveboracensis*, the most common fern in New York."

"Huh? Hey, I see some nuts," says Acky. He bends down to pick them up.

"Those are acorns," says Roger. "You can't eat them."

"Nuts you can't eat, a lake you can't fish in--what kind of place is this anyway?"

I say, "Shut up, asshole."

"Fuck you."

"Don't let my mom hear you say that," says Roger. "Now look at that tree. It's an oak, the kind that acorns grow on. It must be the highest one around. How many feet do you suppose it is?"

"Maybe seventy-five," I say. Acky don't say nothing. He kicks at the ground. *Why did I ever talk him into coming?*

"I'd say eighty," says Roger. "You can tell an oak tree by the shape of the leaves." He goes on giving us a lecture about all the trees and plants till his mother calls us back to eat.

"Now before we sit down," she says, "I'll say grace."

She puts in lots of thees and thous, thanking God for the park and the lake and the trees. "And we thank thee, Lord, for the gift of thy Son, Jesus Christ, who died for our sins--"

This is worse than all the Hail Marys and Our Fathers they made us say in catechism.

"--and may thy Holy Spirit be with our family, and our guests, John and Axel, and our country, and our president, and all those in authority, and all the peoples of the world, for whom thou wast crucified for their sins--"

Ain't she ever gonna stop?

Finally she says, "Amen," and we can eat. She doles out the sandwiches. Acky jams his in his big yap, asking for more with his mouth full.

"I'm sorry, dear. That's all the liverwurst, but we have tuna sandwiches and peanut butter and jelly."

Acky says, "Don't like 'em."

"And there's potato salad and cole slaw and apples."

"You don't like peanut butter?" says Roger. Margie looks at Acky like he's some skunk taking a crap.

Acky's eying the half a liverwurst sandwich I have left on my plate.

"OK, asshole, take it. I'll have a tuna sandwich and some potato salad and cole slaw."

Mrs. Harriet heaps some on my plate, and I thank her. She smiles at me. "I like to see someone who appreciates his food." She looks over at Acky. He's too dumb to get it.

I wonder if Margie is smiling too. She ain't.

I guess I'm not gonna get my cherry broke on this trip.

The Tree

Roger's blabbing about how big the trees are and how some have been there for three thousand years and how they drop shit on the ground and feed themselves.

Wow--three thousand years. Well anyway, the sky gets dark real quick and I hear thunder a long way off.

Margie says, "We better head back." She starts gathering up the stuff and putting it in the basket.

Mrs. Harriet says, "Don't worry, dear. The storm is far away and probably not coming this way."

"Mother. You know how I feel about storms. Roger, help me gather things."

So, like a hero, I say, "I'll climb that tree and see what's up." The tree is huge and I'm starting to think I shot my mouth off. But Margie gives me an almost smile, and I get to thinking where that could lead.

Acky jumps in and says. "I'll go up with you." Acky likes to climb, so this ain't shit to him.

"Find another tree. This one's mine."

So I move up branch by branch. Always making sure I got one foot and one hand on the tree at the same time, like Acky taught me. I'm halfway up, and the wind is blowing, and the sky looks like sewer water. I hear voices down below jumbled up with the wind, telling me to come down, but I keep going.

The tree's humming and bending with the wind. I'm high now. See everything. The lightning flashes followed by thunder. The wall of rain sweeping the treetops, twisting and turning through the valley and over the mountains.

There's a break in the layer of clouds and the blue shows through, and there are rays of light moving across the treetops and the rain falling through, and I feel the vibration of the tree, and I can smell the pine and the rain, and I feel good, and it's got nothing to do with the Holy Spirit.

1952 Executive Meeting

July

The Merry Band is in session around the plywood table top supported by two orange crates. Every once in a while someone, usually Googie, bumps into the contraption and topples it into our laps, so we rarely put our elbows or anything important on it, even ideas.

Googie is filling in Pidgy and me on the gang's latest movie adventure.

"We're in the Lyric watching The Wizard of Oz, and this queer got his hand spidering up my leg--creeping towards my dick. So I ask Hutty to pass me Ginzo's butt. Then Hutty says, 'What you want a butt for?'"

"Nuh-uh, I didn't say nothin' like that. You asked for a butt and I didn't have a clue what you wanted."

"I wanted you to get the dincher from Ginzo down at the end."

Googie says, "Lemme back up and give you guys the big picture. Ginzo is on the last seat--then Acky—then Hutty and me, and we're all watching this movie about this dumb bitch Dorothy, who's wandering around in la-la land looking for her house in some fucked-up place called Kansas."

"The movie was all in black and white, and then it came up in color—weird. What was that thing that took the house away?" says Hutty.

"A tornado, stupid," says Acky.

"Let's get back to the dincher," says Googie. "By the time the butt gets to me, it's all fucked up and smoked down to maybe half an inch—more fire than tobacco--and I squoosh it on the fag's hand and burn the shit out of my fingers. So there we are–me and the queer jumping up and down—me sucking on my fingers and the fag calling me a nasty stinking sonofabitch—and he stands up–and he's a big motherfucker—he's huge—and he looks like he's gonna throw me off the balcony--and he does."

Everybody laughs, and the table falls over into our laps.

We redo our Round Table, and Pidgy says, "Let's call this session to order."

"We need two more orange crates," says Acky.

"Are you making a motion to that effect?" says Pidgy. "Any seconds?"

Pidgy has this little book called *Robert's Rules of Order*, and he always has his beak in it at meetings. So nobody knows what he's talking about most of the time.

"Yeah, I second and third it," says Googie.

Ginzo says, "We need to talk about Johnny wanting to bring spics in."

"We have a motion on the floor—do we have a second?"

"Next thing we let the niggers move in."

Yesterday, I'd let slip the idea of letting Vito and Bernardo join the gang—big mistake.

"Come on, guys, we still have a motion on the table."

I say, "I never said anything about having spics join us."

"What about the motion?" says Pidgy.

"Fuck your motion," says Googie, "What's this about spics?"

Ginzo says," I heard Bo talking to Pidgy saying some shit about his spic friends joining us up."

"No way," says Hutty.

"Don't call me Bo."

"Bo and Pidgy are on the roof playing chess, and I hear them talking about those spics and how they're hot shit."

"You call me Bo one more time and I'll eat your lunch."

"Call to order—we still have a question on the table."

Googie, a little quicker than the rest of us, figures it's a question about the procedure and not the flimsiness of the table. "What's the question?"

"Who the fuck knows?"

"Who the fuck cares?"

1952 Puerto Ricans

July

Me and the guys are sitting on the stoop shooting the shit. The wind is blowing and I can smell the ocean as it squeezes up the street from the river.

Googie says, "You guys see the sign in fronta the Bucket of Blood?"

Ginzo's trying to light up a smoke and the wind don't cooperate. A sheet of newspaper dances over to us and starts twirling around his leg--he kicks it off.

I say, "What sign?"

"The sign in fronta the Bucket of Blood. No Spics Allowed."

Ginzo says, "Yeah, I heard that a longshoreman threw a spic through the window and they hadda board it up."

"Board what up?"

"The window, stupid."

Lenny's scratching his head. "I don't get it."

Lenny's a little slow since he fell off a trolley car.

"The guy live?"

"Who gives a fuck? Right through the plate glass. Sliced him up like baloney," says Googie.

"Who's the owner?" asks Pidgy.

"Who gives two shits?"

"One of the big guys tells me that the Bucket's gonna get ridda the window and just use plywood."

Ginzo says, "Usta be."

"Usta be what?"

"Plywood."

"Who gives a fuck?" says Googie.

"A new spic family moved in upstairs from me," says Lenny.

Googie says, "The spics are taking over--comin' in boatloads. Next thing you know, we'll have to learn spic."

"Fried bananas. They eat these fried bananas," says Lenny.

"Fried bananas? Who the fuck ever heard of frying a banana?"

"You don't wanna get into a scrap with a spic," says Googie. "They all got knives."

"That's a lotta bullshit," says Pidgy. "They're plantains, not bananas, and not all spics carry knives."

"Whatta you know about it?" says Googie. "You some kinda spic lover?"

I say, "They're OK. I had some of those plantains once. Sorta like potatoes in a banana jacket."

Googie says. "Are you eating in a spic's house?"

"Who? Me? No way I'm gonna eat with spics."

Yesterday Vito and his brother Bernardo invited me over to their house for some eats and to meet their mom. The situation was a little iffy since they were Puertos and it would put me on the spic-lover list. But Jesus Christ and Holy Moly, their sister Teresa is gorgeous, so I took Vito up on it. As usual, my dick pointed the way.

Googie says, "The spics are moving in with their big bananas and taking up our pussy."

Acky says, "Nobody'd want that corkscrew dick of yours anyway. Besides if you got you some, you wouldn't know what the fuck to do--you're still a virgin."

"I'm not a virgin."

I say, "You fuckin'-A are."

Googie says "I had a hand job once."

"Angelina? She don't count."

* * * * * * *

Now, Teresa, she's something else--got this little waist you could put your hands around and touch fingers. Then there are those butterfly eyes. Eyes--she gave me the eye once--at least I think she gave me the eye. Maybe she got something caught in it, or maybe she was looking at some asshole behind me. But anyway, she's gorgeous, even though she's a spic. So what do I do? I buddy up with Vito and Bernardo to see if I can get in. Don't ask me what 'in' is--I don't know yet.

So here I am knockin' on Vito's door like I wanna see him. His mom answers and starts talking in Spanish, and I make like I know what she's talking about. I get that she wants me to come in. Teresa is eating at the kitchen tub. Yeah, they got a tub in the kitchen like us--only difference is the icebox--they have a real icebox. Well anyway, she's gorgeous, even when she's eating. She gives me a "Hi," and those butterfly eyes, and I stand there like a dummy, looking around at the walls and my stupid shoes.

"Vito's in the bedroom," says Teresa.

I go into the bedroom and Vito's getting up. He's naked and has this big hard-on--it's huge, curved, and pointing up like a ski jump. God must love Vito to give him a boner like that. I'm a little embarrassed at seeing that thing waving around so I go back into the kitchen to get another look at his sister.

God, is she fine. Hope I don't get a hard-on. Hope my face isn't getting red. Maybe that's good--it'll hide the pimples. Goddamit, why did I hafta think of pimples? Now she'll see it for sure--under the Clearasil--that big fuck on the end of my nose.

She smiles at me. I feel my pants rising.

"I'll wait outside."

"You can wait here."

I say, "No, that's OK," and take my nose and dick out into the hallway.

1952 Hell's Kitchen Aerodynamics

July

Me, Pidgy, and Acky are on the floor in the living room. The army cots are pushed aside, and we're huddled over the P51. We've been working on the stick and paper fighter for months. The floor around us is messy with balsa wood; the smell of airplane glue is strong. I'm doing some final touches on the twelve-inch wing.

Richie's trying to sleep. Ma just gave him one of his fit pills and he's humming and banging his head on the pillow.

"The wing first," I say.

"Nuh-uh, let's work on the body," says Acky.

I say, "Wings."

"Body. We need to finish the body before we can do the wings."

"I wanna do the wings."

Ma's in the doorway watching. "Stop fighting. You boys need to clean up that mess."

"We will, Ma--when we finish."

"The body," says Acky.

"It's called a fuselage," says Pidgy.

"The directions say the wings--we do the wings first." I take them down from a hook and wire on the ceiling.

Acky gets the body down. "You got to finish the fusi-lodge first 'cause that's the way it's done," he says.

Pidgy gets his two cents in--and adds a dime. "You must keep overall weight to a minimum and plan for proper balance without ballast while beefing up landing gear, motor mounting, wing structure and--"

"Huh?"

"We have to look more into our power source. Acky's idea of using rubber power may not get it off the ground."

"Rubber power?"

"Rubber bands."

"What the fuck you know about it?" says Acky.

"It's all about aerodynamics--things like power and lift. For example the Baby Spitfire gas engine uses a glow plug--"

"Why not use a steam engine?"

"Ha, ha, very funny."

Richie's still pounding his head.

"Will you boys shut up. He needs to sleep."

Little Charley is sitting on the tub. He starts banging on it with a spoon.

"Stop that," says Ma.

Pidgy continues. "Back to the glow plug, which keeps the weight down, since you don't need an electrical system-- battery and all that stuff."

"The plan says we can do it with rubber power," says Acky.

"Never get off the ground--look at the size."

Richie wakes up and starts to cry. From the kitchen, Ma says, "If you kids don't quiet down, I'll throw that plane out the window."

Nobody moves. She says, "Go outside and play."

I say, "No, Ma, we'll be good."

Outside don't work for us. Me and Acky are waiting for the old man to come home so's we can mooch some money offa him.

Acky turns up the radio.

> *Pepsi Cola hits the spot.*
> *Twelve full ounces--that's a lot.*
> *Twice as much for a nickel too.*
> *Pepsi Cola is the drink for you.*

"What're you kids doing now?" says Ma.

"We ain't doing nothing, Ma. Just fooling around."

"I don't want you bothering Richie."

I say, "He's OK--he went back to sleep."

"Keep the noise down, or I'll have to lock you in the bathroom."

"It's time for the Lone Ranger," says Pidgy.

"We need to work on the plane."

"But we're outta glue."

"Besides the radio won't reach--the wire's too short."

"Yeah, it only works on the tub."

"We need more balsa wood."

"We know that. This is just a planning thing."

"But we're missing The Lone Ranger."

"Fuck the Long Ranger and Pronto," says Acky. He still can't get it right.

We work on the plane for a while, mostly doing nothing but talking about how the wings might fall off or how it might fly off and disappear or maybe get shot down by some Nip over Mt Fuji.

Finally the old man comes home--all filled up. He ain't real happy about us with a plane in the middle of the living room and Richie banging his head against the wall, and Charley whining.

"Wazzahell's going on here--this place is a dessasster." He picks up a chair, props it against the entry door knob, and gives it a kick to snug it up. "Can't a guy come home to a li'l peazand quiet? Damn barrrtender, e'rey budy wantz money." He trips over his own feet, passing out before he hits the kitchen floor.

Ma says, "Leave him there. Just push him next to the tub so we can get through."

1952 The Flight from Hell's Kitchen

July

I say, "You're nuts. Van Cortlandt Park on roller skates? It's two hundred blocks."

"I did it in four hours," says Acky.

"On a bike."

"Dumb idea."

Pidgy's painting the other wing. "If we take the subway, we can get there in less than an hour."

"Maybe we can get us some money changing bottles. Rent bikes," says Acky.

"Why do you always wanna do it different?" I say. "Everything I wanna do you don't."

"We take the IRT and we're there in an hour," says Pidgy.

I say, "How about we tie the plane to the handlebars and wait for a head wind and you can fly there."

Acky says, "Add a little nitro to the gas and you'll get there in five seconds. Kaffooom."

"Actually, nitroglycerin can be added to the methanol to increase power and to make the engine easier to start," says Pidgy.

I say, "And maybe blow us all up. Why don't we go to Central Park? Then our families won't have to go too far to collect the parts."

"Very funny."

"Nuh-uh--we need a real landing field. I vote for Van Cortlandt," says Acky.

I say, "We gotta go through Harlem to get there."

Acky says, "Nigger City. I ain't afraid of no niggers."

Pidgy's painting the last letter on the plane's wing, spelling out THE ROBBIN' HOODS. "If it gets into an updraft, we'll be shit outta luck."

"Maybe it'll rain."

"Wind can be a problem."

"Can we get it in the subway?"

"Should we take the wings off?"

"That's nuts."

"Central Park."

"Van Cortlandt."

"Maybe it won't start?"

"Let's just take it up on the roof and test the motor."

"Where do we buy nitro?"

* * * * * * *

"Two hundred blocks on the IRT ain't bad," says Pidgy.

"Unless you're going through a nigger neighborhood carrying a two-foot airplane," says Acky.

Pidgy has the plane on his lap. Me and Acky are sitting on both sides of him, sprawling our legs to keep the crowd from knocking the tail off. The train stops at Harlem.

There's three of 'em, a little nasty-looking kid with a wide mouth, and two frizzy-haired bodyguards. The two frizzies are big. They sit on the other side and give us banana split smiles. I think maybe we can handle them. They're about our age.

"Hey, white boy, what you got there?" says Big Mouth, propped up by his bodyguards.

I knew this was gonna happen.

"What's it to you, black boy?" says Acky. I coulda predicted that too. My brother thinks he's invincible.

Pidgy says, "It's a Fokker 272, powered by a 172 Messerschmitt."

"Are you Fokkers fokking with us?" says Big Mouth.

Why is it always the little guy with the big mouth?

Frizzy Right says. "The skinny guy with the plane looks like a chicken." The three of them laugh. Pidgy hugs the plane.

"Careful." says Frizzy Left. "You'll break your chicken wings."

Acky's ready to rumble. Pidgy wants to fly. Maybe we wanna talk this thing down.

I say, "We ain't looking for trouble."

The passengers around us start moving away like they don't wanna get involved. Pansy asses.

Pointing at the writing on the plane, Big Mouth says, "Looka that. The punks thinks they's Robin Hood's mob."

Now this is starting to get me pissed off, the cocksuckers calling us punks and fucking with our name.

Acky says, "Did you call us punks?"

"What you say?"

I nudge Acky. He ignores it.

Pidgy wraps his arms around the plane and wants to be somewhere else.

The crowd moves back farther.

They got on at 125th. The park is on 246th St. How many blocks is that?

The train stops at 168th St. More of them get on. Subtraction problem: what's 168 from 246? Maybe a half hour to go.

Pickin' on Pidgy, Frizzy Left says, "Smack his ass to the promised land."

Frizzy Right says, "I don't mean to be mean, but yo' momma need Listerine--not a sip, not a swallow, but the whole damn bottle."

I say, "You guys ain't poets, and you don't know it, and the words don't show it."

Big Mouth says, "You chickens are slim pickin's."

These guys are pretty good. Too bad Googie ain't here-- we'd clobber them.

I say, "I'll give you a dime if you quit the rhyme."

Acky says, "Your mother's so nice she'd give me the hair off her back."

"Yo' momma smell like ass crack," says Big Mouth.

I say, "Your mother's so nice I love her."

Terrible. Why couldn't Googie be here?

"Yo' Momma so nice, all my friends think so too," says Frizzy Right.

"Yo' Momma so nice, she blew me for a nickel," says Frizzy Left, looking at me.

Big Mouth says,

> Why yo' Momma on my nuts?
> She the queen of ho-ville sluts.
> Would you come an' get her please?
> How she love that gov'ment cheese.

Ticking me off, but not bad. Acky's getting red.

I give them a poem back. "Roses are red, and lemons are sour. How much does your mother charge for an hour?"

Frizzy Left leads with a left. "One good snap deserves another--between my legs you'll find your mother."

Frizzy Right leads with a right, " Roses are red, violets are black--why is yo' momma on her back?

> Yo' momma so sick
> She need some dick,
> But she get perfection
> With my injection.

I say,

> Roses are red
> Violets are blue
> Your mother's a chicken
> Any cock'll do.

Acky says, "Your mother wears combat boots." They all roll their eyes at that. It's embarrassing.

"Fuck you--you niggers," says Acky. He's giving them points and pushing us into the shit pile.

Pidgy is all into hugging his plane and don't say nothing, so they start on Acky, calling him a chickenshit crybaby, and that pisses me off. But we luck out--we're saved by the last stop in Harlem.

"Sorry, honkies," says Big Mouth, "We'll have to fart and dart." And he does, and it don't smell like airplane glue.

They get off laughing, like we lost. I give them the finger through the window; they return me some hand jive that I can't translate.

* * * * * * *

"See what I mean," says Acky, "I told you Van Cortlandt Park was the place."

I gotta admit in this case, him and Pidgy were right. Not too many trees to crash into and lotsa open space to lose the plane.

"What if it gets into the buildings?"

"We limit the amount of gas we put in the tank--so that ain't happening," says Pidgy.

"What if the wind takes it away?"

"Flying is a risky business."

Acky says, "We shoulda maked a boat instead."

Pidgy's putting gas in the tank. "We coulda put a radio control system on board, but that costs. Here, Acky, you hold it, and I'll get the engine going,"

"What'll I do if it starts?"

I say, "Throw the fuckin' thing."

Pidgy says, "Just hand it back to me, and I'll take over."

Pidgy gives the prop a turn and it sputters--gives it another and--it sputters again. Now he gives the prop a shitload of turns, and all he gets is sputters and coughs.

"We might have a clogged fuel line."

"Maybe you don't have enough nitro?"

"Did you check the glow plug?"

I say, "This is shit. We come all the way out here, and the plane don't start. Put some nitro in it."

Tourists are starting to gather around us to get a laugh. Pidgy is still cranking the prop. Every once in a while the engine coughs and sputters, bringing in more people. Now they're laughing and pointing at the three dum-dums.

"Goddamn it, Pidgy. Put nitro in the sonofabitch."

Pidgy puts a drop in the tank. It don't do nothing. Sput, sput--all the fuckin' thing does is sput.

"We shoulda done a boat," says Acky.

"Give it more."

"It'll blow the engine."

Acky says, "More."

I say, "More."

Some kid in the crowd says, "More."

"OK," says Pidgy, "but this is not my idea."

The tourists and their kids are milling around, waiting for action. You'd think we were the Wright brothers.

Pidgy adds three more drops into the tank. A kid says, "That's nitro they're putting in the tank." The mob moves back. Pidgy takes a whack at the prop, and the motor gets to screaming. Kids are covering their ears. Acky hangs on to the screaming plane--his eyes are getting bigger, his mouth smaller.

"What the fuck do I do with it?"

I say, "Throw the sonofabitch."

"Give it to me," says Pidgy. "Not propeller first, dummy--tail first."

"Fuck you guys," says Acky and lets it go. The plane climbs a hundred feet--two hundred feet. Suddenly it jumps into an updraft that carries it into the sun. It shrinks into nothing, taking the sound with it.

"What the fuck," says Acky. "Where'd it go?"

"Into the sun."

I say, "It's coming back. I can hear the motor. It's getting louder."

"Where?"

"There, there. In the sun. It's a bird, it's a plane, it's a kamikaze."

"Where?"

"Stop the bullshit--it's gone."

"I don't see nothing."

The tourists, eyes to the sky, start milling around, spreading out.

The kamikaze scream gets louder.

I say, "There, there. It's heading straight for your head."

Some guy says, "I see it. I see it."

A running woman, her arms shielding her head, says, "Oh, my God, I'm going to die."

I say, "Outta the way. Let the lady out. She's in ground zero."

The crowd, looking upward, is frozen in the grass--waiting. Waiting.

* * * * * * * *

Pidgy's sitting between me and Acky, his shoulders bouncing back and forth, and he ain't smiling. The plane, its tail dangling off his knees, wiggles and wobbles as he tries to hold it together.

Pidgy says, "The engine is still good; we just need to do some body work."

The subway emerges from the tunnel into the light and climbs up over the city. The brownstone buildings go by in a blur.

Acky says, "I've had it with the airplane business."

I say, "Why don't we change the subject?"

Acky says, "Why don't we do a boat?"

"The fuselage needs some work, and we can--"

"A boat would be good. We could bring it down to the docks and put it in the Hudson. Or play with it in the park lake."

I say, "Yeah, maybe we can play with it in the kitchen tub." The conversation is boring me, so I start my yawning gimmick.

"Quit that. You're making me yawn," says Acky. He yawns. A girl across from us yawns. Some guy looking at her yawns. I keep yawning, and it spreads like the pox. I can hear it creeping into the next car as it slowly moves toward the conductor, and he falls asleep and we all die, bouncing into brownstones and the rubble of the underpass.

"Really, guys. We can salvage the plane. I got plenty of balsa wood, and the superstructure is fine--maybe a week's work."

I'm looking at the yawning girl across from us and she has these little tits that kinda curve up nice. Her legs are crossed so I don't see nothing there.

I wonder if Acky gets hard-ons yet? That would be fucked up.

The subway slides into the tunnel, and the moving faces and bodies change at each stop. Every once in a while the lights go out, and the sparks from the third rail flash-- freezing the zombies in the dark.

The train lurches, rolls, and rocks towards Times Square. It's getting crowded. A fat guy gets in front of Pidgy. He's holding onto the overhead handle, and his belly's jiggling to the beat of the train.

"What you got there, Sonny?" says Fatso.

Acky says, "What's it to ya?"

Pidgy says, "It's a Fokker 272, powered by a 172 Messerschmitt."

"Looks like you had a problem."

Fatso looks like a good guy, even though he's old like our dad. You can tell a guy is OK by the crinkles on his face-- up is good, and down means he's a creep. Fatso has these big dimples like he smiles a lot, which of course crinkles him in the right direction.

Funny how his belly bounces and jiggles around--maybe he's a clown in a circus or something.

"Don't tell him shit," says Acky.

"Why don't you knock off the lip?" I say.

"I was a pilot during the war."

It must've been driving a bomber; that's the only thing that could've got off the ground with him in it.

"Me and the guys are into airplanes 'cause we wanna be pilots or engineers," says Pidgy.

"You can learn a lot with model planes. I made them as a boy. In the service I began as a flight mechanic and worked myself up to officer training and then ultimately a pilot in the Pacific war."

"Wow," says Pidgy, "Maybe you can give me some ideas on how we can fix this?" The guy looks at the plane like it was his mother in a coffin.

Acky says, "We don't want his two cents."

I say, "Maybe the guy has some ideas."

Acky says, "The plane idea sucks. The fuckin' thing went straight up and came straight down. We'd've had better luck if we tossed a hotdog into the air."

Fatso the Pilot says, "What kind of pins did you use when you put your plane together?"

"Pins?"

The Pilot looks shook up that Pidgy don't know about pins.

"How long did it take you to build that plane?"

"About three months."

"And you didn't use pins?"

"Whaddya think--we're in the pin business?" says Acky.

I get it. We shoulda used pins. No wonder it took us three months--us holding each of them damn sticks till the glue dried.

"You can't use just any pins with balsa construction. There's three types--straight pins, T-pins, and dressmaker pins.

"Which should we use?" says Pidgy.

"T-pins are the best for modelling--they cost quite a bit more, but they excel in what they do, and they're also a lot safer due to the unique folded head. Invest in at least 100 of these in a container--"

"We're going into the boat business," says Acky. "We don't need pins."

"Don't put pins into your framework when you're constructing built-up wings, fuselage sides, and tail feathers. The reason is that the pins crush and damage the wood, the very wood that you're relying on to stay together in flight--"

The train bumps, rattles, and twists along, the Fat Pilot nodding us to numbness with his pointless pins. The doors slide open, and the zombies move in, pushing and jamming in waves.

Last stop, Times Square. More zombies.

"Watch out for my plane."

"Get back, you cocksucker."

The Fat Pilot starts to lose hold and falls on Pidgy. Pidgy slips me the plane. It's knocked outta my hand. Me and the Fat Pilot shove back at the crowd. My wing is knocked off-- the P51 is doomed.

Acky laughs as the plane is trampled and smashed and dragged across the subway floor. "I told you we shoulda done a boat."

1952 Sex Education

July

"Wait'll I get my hands on Acky."

"What about the park? We were supposed to be going to the park," says Pidgy.

"Ten bucks--he took ten dollars. My mother won't be able to get the groceries. No liverwurst."

"Let's go to the park?"

"Can't you see my family's gonna starve?"

Acky's always into something--can't keep his hands offa things--but going into Ma's purse'll get his ass kicked. You don't steal money off your mother.

Pidgy says, "Where the hell is Acky?"

I say, "Maybe he's on a roof? or in a basement?"

"Looka the weather, Bo. No wind--perfect for the park."

"Yeah, yeah--and don't call me Bo."

"Yeah, yeah. Sorry, Bo--I mean Johnny."

Where's Acky? Gotta get him before he spends the money.

Googie comes outta the alley.

"You see Acky?"

It's not too smart of me, asking Googie for help.

Googie says, "Yeah, I saw Acky, and you don't wanna know what he's up to."

It's dumb to ask Googie a question and lay yourself open. Googie's good at repeating shit like that to get your head all fucked up.

He points at a nearby fruit truck with a canvas back. "Your queer brother's in there with Jimmy Jones."

"Jimmy Jones?"

"They're playing with each other."

"Playing what?"

"It's a jerk-off circle--the little guys have been shaking hands with shorty all day. Your brother and Jimmy Jones started the action. Far as I know they're still in there."

I don't believe it. Acky jerking off Jimmy Jones. A Fleming, jerking off the biggest prick in the block? My brother a queer?

I approach the canvas and don't wanna open it. The truck is vibrating. I can hear a fast clicking noise and then panting. I can't resist--so I peek.

Holy shit, it's Acky's hand, and it's moving faster and faster. I can't take my eyes offa it. Jimmy Jones's groin's pumping and humping. "Ahh, ahh." He's ready to let loose. I never seen it squirt so far. It's all over Acky's hand, and I'm fascinated with the shiny, white cum. I get a hard-on, and I'm pissed.

Oh, my god, I'm a queer too.

1952 The Business of the Butts

July

It's late evening and we're having our usual smoke under the lamp post. Most of the street noise is gone for the day. Old Lady Piper, our neighborhood snoop cop, leans out her window and shouts at some kids below, "You boys better go home. It's getting late." The kids move off into the darkness laughing.

It's our time to shoot the shit, have a smoke, maybe do a little slipping.

"Why don't we all chip in and buy a pack? How much do you guys have?" says Googie.

Most of the kids can't afford a full pack of cigarettes. We pick up dinchers off the street if the smoker was nice enough to leave a large one and shoe stomp, not smear. I collect these gems and store them in one of my old man's tobacco tins and maybe later use them for trade or roll-your-owns.

One day Googie picked up something that turned out not to be a large cigar stub and the word got around to stay clear of him for a while. Dinchers are a chancy business, so we're on the lookout for a new opportunity.

Pidgy, a major James Dean nut, always reminds us how he looks like James Dean, combs his hair like Dean; has seen every movie he made; and cried when Turnipseed crashed into his Spyder and killed him.

Pidgy says, "Why don't we start rolling our own?" Then, as usual, he answers the question before we can say no. "It's cheap--tobacco and paper are about a quarter of the cost of a factory smoke, and besides we can save the dinchers and add them to the rolling tobacco. Bo is doing that now."

Pidgy, head tilted back, is comb whipping his hair into nasty waves for the deep look, the roll-your-own hanging from his mouth, all dead giveaways to his idol. "Roll-your-owns are the coming thing. We gotta be the guys that set the trends in the block. Fresh tobacco, the experience we get rolling them, the show we could put on making them. And what about the wow factor with the girls--they'll be falling all over themselves to get into our pants."

"Fuck James Dean." says Googie. "He probably died in his Porsche rolling one of those fucking cigarettes. Roll-your-owns suck. The tobacco dries up and smokes like shit on a stick; every time the wind blows, I'm blinded and buried in the crap. And when I light the fucking things, they bust into flames and torch the hairs outta my nose. Fuck them and your fucking comb."

Pidgy is shocked by this attack on his idol and his hair. "You ain't no Frank Sinatra."

"That's lame," I say.

Skinny says, "Who the hell told you that you look like James Dean? Get the lard outta your hair and lose the comb. The girls are running away."

The evening slipping session has started; it looks like a good one; Googie and Skinny are the best on the block.

After a few hours the James Dean roll-your-owns is dead. Lenny brings up the idea of ripping off the big guys.

"I started lifting butts from my big brother--just a few so he wouldn't notice. That worked real good until I took too much, and he kicked my ass and started tucking them in his T-shirt sleeve and sleeping with them."

"That's why we call him Dirty Dan," I say. "His ear smells like shit whenever he takes the cotton out."

"Lay off," says Lenny.

"Great idea" says Googie. "The Robbin' Hoods rob off the rich big guys and get our asses kicked. You and your brother have shit for brains. Gimme a smell." Googie moves closer to Lenny, trying to smell his ear. Lenny pushes him away. "Maybe we can get all the big guys to tuck their cigs into their dirty T-shirts so they can parade a fucking Ringling Brothers Circus of cigarettes up and down 47th Street for us to rob them."

"Fuck you, you gimp."

* * * * * * *

So I speak to Sal, the corner candy store owner, about a profitable business we can set up.

"Sal, you sell Luckies for twenty cents a pack and Wings for fifteen--right?"

"What are you getting at?"

"If I could show you how to sell Wings for twenty cents a pack, would you be interested?"

"Of course."

"You break open a pack of Wings and sell them to us for a penny apiece."

"Go on."

"I have a shitload of customers who'll buy them as loosies—you get them hooked on Wing loosies at a penny each and move them up to Luckies at a cent and a half or two cents apiece. Just break up a few packs of Wings and leave them in a shoebox –no labor involved. I'll spread the word and send every kid in the block to you--you'll make a fortune."

"What do you get for this idea?"

"Let me show you what I can do, and maybe we can make a special deal for me."

Sal likes this idea, and he slips me a pack every once in a while.

1952 Baloney and Cheese

July

It all started with cheese. Maybe it was a package of cream cheese. Maybe a block of cheddar. I never saw it.

Acky runs into the flat, slams the door shut, and jumps on his bed. He's outta breath.

Ma says, "What did you do?"

"Nothing. I didn't do nothing."

He looks scared shit--like he wants to crawl under his bed.

I say, "What did you do?"

There's banging on the door. Someone in the courtyard yells, "The cops are going into 32."

Richie says, "What did you do?"

More banging on the door. "Open up. This is the police."

Acky says, "Shit--shit--shit." Pulls his blanket over his head.

Charley says, "What did you do?"

The cops take Acky away.

1952 The Police Station

July

We've been at the police station for three hours. Me, Charley, and Richie are antsy. Ma, as usual, has the patience of a stone.

"I'm sorry, ma'am. I know it was only a block of cheese, but Axel has priors and we have to hold him till he sees the judge."

"But he's such a good boy--never gets into trouble. He goes to church--he has good grades."

I can't believe she said that.

Charley, hiding behind her, snot dripping from his nose, says, "Mommy, Mommy."

Richie says, "I wanna go home. I don't like this place." He's tugging at her dress. She pats him on the dome and says, "If you're good boys, I'll make you liverwurst sandwiches when we get home."

Two flatfoots bring in an old guy and this kid about my age. The old guy has a bandage on his hand.

"The little bastard stabbed me. I want to press charges."

"What's the story," says the Desk to the kid.

"I'm in this movie, and this queer--" He points at him. "--slides his hand up my leg."

"He's lying. I never touched him."

"Let the boy talk."

"Then he grabs me by the cock, so I stab him."

Cool.

"Take 'em back to the tank," says the Desk.

As they go through the doorway, I can hear voices. Someone says, "When the hell do we get to eat? Is there a lunch?"

Then I hear some scuffling and maybe a fight.

The Desk gets up and yells, "Shut the fuck up, or I'll bring in the hose."

Acky's back there with a bunch of queers and crooks.

"Mommy, I don't like this place. I'm hungry," says Richie. Charley's yanking on her dress.

Ma pours it on, tears floating up to the desk cop, "Don't worry," she says. "Everything will be all right. The nice policeman will let Axel go home with us." She takes out a Kleenex and wipes her eyes, then Charley's nose. *Good thing she didn't do it the other way around.*

A cop comes in with a couple of girls. They're wearing tight skirts, and their knockers are hanging out. Lots of make-up, a dead giveaway. The Desk motions them through the doorway.

No check-in at the desk? Maybe they have reservations.

Richie, parked on a nearby bench, is rocking back and forth, mumbling, cooking up one of his fits.

This sucks--surrounded by cops and bums, Charley crying, Ma crying, and Richie soon to be flopping around on the floor like a landed fish. I don't know whether I want to laugh or cry.

I say to Ma, "Richie's about to have a fit. We need to go home."

"What's wrong with you? What kind of person are you? Your brother's in jail and maybe going to prison, and you want to just leave him here?"

"I didn't say that." *She's right. That's exactly what I want. Dumb bastard deserves it.*

I say, "Look, Richie's mumbling and rocking."

"He does that all the time."

"Now he's starting to do the twitches."

The Desk cop looks bored, on the phone talking, listening, mumbling to assholes, robbing time from the real people. And me--us--standing there taking it.

A new flatfoot drags in this guy wearing a zoot suit. Unbelievable--a bright green zoot suit--baggy pants, pistol pockets, and a porkpie hat--even a long gold chain for twirling keys. Zoot is in cuffs, and Flatfoot pushes him up to the desk.

"I didn't do it," says Zoot.

"What's the charge?" asks the Desk.

"Indecent exposure and resisting arrest."

"Not guilty," says Zoot. "It was a 'mergency."

Desk says "Put him in the cage. We'll give him a strip search and see what his drawers look like."

Flatfoot yanks and pushes Zoot towards the door of voices.

"It was a 'mergency. I hadda go. I was waiting for my girl."

This guy with a girl. Unbelievable.

"I'm not guilty." Both cops are laughing.

Ma says, "What about Axel?"

"Sorry, Ma'am. You'll have to wait. Lunchtime." He breaks open a bag and starts stuffing a baloney sandwich into his face.

Charley says, "Mommy, I'm hungry."

Ma, the rock, says, "It'll be just a little longer."

1952 The Hospital

August

I was thirteen when my mother and dad and I went to St. Vincent's Hospital to talk to the surgeon about getting my leg straight. They had heard of a free treatment program there for conditions like mine.

The doctor is a Chink; his face is round, his hands long. Great for surgery, I hope.

"We don't have any money," Ma says.

"Don't worry; it's all part of Saint Vincent's Education and Training program."

The doctor makes me take my pants off and looks at my leg.

"What caused that?" asks my old man.

"It looks like a case of Blount's Disease," says the doctor. "We don't know what causes it, but it's most often found in Negroes. The inner part of the tibia, just below the knee, fails to develop normally, causing angulation of the bone."

"Negroes? What do we have to do with Negroes?"

"I've worked in colored communities and have seen many cases, but this is the first time I've experienced it in a Caucasian."

"He wouldn't drink his milk," says Dad. "Could that have been the cause?"

"No," says the doctor. "That might cause rickets, but this isn't rickets." He holds my leg in both hands and manipulates it left and right, checking to see how loose it is.

"We now know it's not an inherited disease, but it could have something to do with early walking," says the doctor.

"I told you," says Dad. "You shouldn'a let him start so early."

"How could I stop him?" says Ma.

"When did he start walking?" asks the doctor.

"He was six months old--he never walked; he ran like a bear on all fours and then stood up and ran faster. He never stopped. I couldn't keep up with him," says Dad.

"That's the earliest case I've heard of. Usually they're at least nine months old."

"I knew he was special," says Dad.

"The thing to do now is figure out how to correct it. We shouldn't have any problem straightening out that left leg. The right one is a little bowed, but there'll be no need to operate on that."

"We'll have to break it here." He points to an area four inches below my left knee. "And we'll need to put a pin through the tibia about here." He points a little lower.

"Pin?" I say. My stomach does flip-flops. *Maybe I don't want to do this*.

"A stainless steel rod narrower than a pencil. It goes through the bone to keep the lower part of your leg in the new straightened position. Then we put the cast on to lock it until it sets."

"How long does the cast stay on?" I ask.

"About eight weeks."

"How big is the cast?"

"Up to your hip."

"Up to my hip?"

"We need to keep the leg immobile at the knee. Restrict movement to keep it straight for you. Don't worry, we'll have you up and running in a few months, and your leg will be as straight as an arrow."

* * * * * * *

I wake up and try to roll over, but I can't. I look at my leg, a cast up to the hip, hot and heavy. I wiggle my toes to see if they're alive. They move--the leg's still connected. I'm numb and groggy. I doze off again and dream–a dark turban and a flashing scimitar in the dark behind me moving fast--me running--me falling and whack–off with the leg.

I wake up, grabbing the cast, grabbing the leg. It's there! It's there! Holy shit--I thought it was gone. I doze off again, hoping for better dreams.

I wake up again to some old fart complaining in the bed next to me while a guy in a white coat is sticking a tube in his dick.

"Ooohhh," the old man says.

White Coat says, "I'm having trouble getting it in, Pete."

"Well hurry it up. Jam the damn thing in there—this is not an enjoyable experience."

"I can't get it past the prostate—wait, I think I got it." White Coat finally inserts the tube with an attached bag and opens a valve.

"Ahhhhhhh, thank God! I thought I was going to explode."

The bag fills up quickly, and White Coat helps him empty it. "Wow, in twenty years I've never seen so much come out so fast."

"I've been dribbling for months."

"We'll need to leave the catheter in until the operation. Please let me know if there is any discomfort."

"You must be kidding."

While there's a small break in the action, I say, "I'm starting to have a little pain. Can I have a pill or something?"

"Sorry, son, you'll have to ask your nurse for that when she comes. But I'll mention it to her when I'm finished here."

I say, "Thanks." The cast is warm and getting hotter.

There's a cork or something on both sides of my leg—reminds me of the electrodes on Frankenstein's head. I grab hold of one and wiggle it to see if the other side moves. Probably not a good idea, but I do it anyway. It moves, and I wonder if that's a good or bad sign. *Does it go through the leg or around the leg? Maybe I should leave it alone. What does the wiggling mean?*

White Coat soon leaves, after putting all his tools away. Pete says, "What a relief. I haven't been able to piss for days."

"That's tough, Pops." The leg's starting to hurt more, and Pete's beginning to bug me with his dick problem. I call out to one of the passing nurses and ask her for something for the pain. She just keeps walking.

"Just you wait, sonny. The day'll come when they'll be sticking tubes in every hole you have."

"Yeah, yeah."

Pete realizes I'm not fully operational, so he shuts up for a while.

The pain in the leg starts to throb. Apparently whatever they gave me during the operation is wearing off. "Where is that nurse? I need an aspirin or something. This shit is starting to hurt."

Pete calls out towards the hall, "Nurse, nurse."

They keep walking by. I hear their white shoes squeaking. Pete keeps pushing his buzzer. I start pushing mine. Nobody comes.

Pete says, "This place is the shits. No service, crappy food, and high prices."

Finally a nurse dressed in sparkling white enters with her starched cap. Her pumping breasts are huge. "What's the commotion here?"

I want to give her hell for not coming sooner. But I'm a prisoner.

"Could I have an aspirin or something? The leg is hurting."

"I'm sorry I can't give you anything until the prescribed time."

"But it hurts."

"You'll have to wait a few more hours, as per doctor's orders." She takes her tits and the little white cap into the hallway and disappears.

My ma and dad show up regularly with pizza and comic books. Ma is upset about the operation, blaming herself for all the pain I'm going through. Hoping it wasn't a mistake. The old man don't say much, but I think he's proud of me for taking it like a man.

* * * * * * *

It's been three days since I took a crap, so I think I'll give it another try. The problem is my huge cast dangling so I can't get my ass high enough to slide on the pan.

While doing this balancing act for the third time, I remember the time Acky had a similar problem.

He came home one day and showed me his fist split wide open at the knuckle.

"How'd you do that?" I said.

"I got me into a fight with Lenny, hit the bastard right in his rotten teeth."

"Wow. That looks mean. You'll need to get that stitched up."

"I'll be all right. Don't tell the old man." Acky's terrified of doctors. He'll dive off the Queen Mary, but doctors and hospitals scare the hell out of him. "I'll just give it a few days. It's looking better already."

Three days later he had a swollen, pus-filled hand with a red line going up his arm and a doctor telling him, "One more day and I would've had to take this hand off."

Two more days in the hospital, holding it back, hoping, praying that he could go home to finally take a shit. The mountain became unsurmountable, and he had to do it in the deadly embarrassing bedpan.

Once the prize was there—too ashamed to present this huge aromatic bundle to a nurse, he installed it in a paper bag and tossed it out the window. Acky's bombing mission went on for several days while the unused bedpan, to the staff's puzzlement, glistened cleanly in the cabinet.

I too don't want the shame of doing it in a bedpan. But I'm unwilling to go to Acky's extreme. So there I am, balanced on this cold bedpan grunting and swearing. Talk about shitting a brick. Wow--I'm putting up a new building.

There is nothing like the ecstasy of a good crap.

* * * * * * *

Guess what? The fat Asian doctor with the magic hands and his crew have screwed up.

"We need to redo the procedure—it's not quite straight."

"Is this a joke?" says my old man. My mother starts crying. It's been a week, the pain's gone, and they want to do it all over again.

My old man is pissed. He starts mumbling a lot of nasty shit in Italian; then he does it in Spanish. Lucky for the doc Pops can't speak Chinese.

"It shouldn't take long—we can do it tomorrow morning." He holds out a form to my mom and dad. "Could you please sign this. I'll need your permission." We all look at each other, boxed in by this incredible Chinaman and the incredible dilemma he's put us into.

Resigned, my parents sign.

In the morning, they roll me off the bed onto a gurney and wheel me into the operating room. A different doc, a younger one with buck teeth, is there amid his shiny tools. "I'm Dr. Hackenburg. I'll be doing the procedure this morning. Don't worry--it shouldn't take long." He smiles.

Where's the first doctor? Who is this guy?

The hacksaw stands out. I wonder how many legs it's cut off. Dr. Hacksaw then takes some kind of ruler and draws lines on my cast. Finishing his artwork, he picks up this huge syringe with a needle the size of an ice pick and says, "This is going to hurt a little. Roll over on your side." He and the nurse help prop my whole leg to get my ass and back positioned.

That done, he swabs my back and starts sticking the pick in my spine. It hurts like hell. I move a little, can't help it.

He says, "Don't move. This is very important. You could be paralyzed if you do."

Here I am with Dr. Hacksaw sticking an ice pick in my back, my leg in a cast up to my hip, and him telling me not to move or be paralyzed for life. *When does the good news start?*

All that done, he helps me to roll over on my back again, not knowing if I'm temporarily paralyzed or in a more permanent state. He pulls out the saw, and I wonder how far it will go into my leg. Putting that aside, he grabs this motorized thing with a wheel on the end and starts zipping away just below the Frankenstein pin, and I wonder if he's gonna cut my leg off.

Dust flies every which way as the disk whines, the doc's face covered by a plastic shield. Now with my leg cast cut in half, they strap the upper part of me and the cast to the table, and then the doc grabs the lower half of my leg and twists it till something snaps, and it ain't only the cast. Paralyzed, I feel nothing.

"Done. Straight as an arrow. Tape him up."

I wake up to a repeat performance of my hospital life skit, my leg in the air, me groggy and waiting for the pain.

Pete is fiddling with his urine bag. "Dammit, how much longer do I have to wear this thing?"

White Coat says, "It's only been three days since your surgery. You're supposed to wear it for at least a week."

"I'm getting sore right here." He points at his lower back.

White Coat takes out a thermometer and says, "Roll over." After a few minutes he looks at it and says, "I'll have to talk to the doctor."

"What is it? What's the matter?"

"Your temperature is a little bit elevated."

"How high is it?"

"101.5"

"I knew it. I knew it. Something's wrong. My kidney's infected. You'd better get me something for it."

"Take it easy, Pete. You know I'll have to get the doctor's OK, and your temperature isn't that high. Maybe it's from that pastrami sandwich."

Apparently White Coat and Pete are a comedy team. Pete, the full-time patient, and White Coat, his straight man. The old guy talks all the time about his ailments--bad kidneys, memory loss, crunching back, and popcorn knees.

* * * * * * *

Comics are a fast read; therefore Ma can't keep up with me on the delivery end. I'm back into the pain business, so I need them for distraction. As soon as she brings a stack of super heroes collected from Pidgy, I read them and ask for more; and of course, considering the situation and her guilt, I exploit her. Every day she brings another stack. I become the hospital joke. White Coat, Pete, and Big Tits call me the Comic Book Kid. My father, who can't read, ignores me but sneaks in a pizza every once in a while.

"Why don't you graduate?" says Pete.

"Graduate?"

"Don't you notice the book cart that goes down the hall every day?"

"Yeah, so what?"

"Did you ever read a book?"

"Sure."

I've read lots of books in school, and most of them sucked: *The Red Pony, Black Beauty*. All horseshit on concrete.

"Why don't you check it out? You're wearing your mother out running for comic books."

Pete's OK once he stops talking about his dick. I appreciate his attempt to help, but books are dense for me, no pictures, no action, no imagination, very little information on a page. Boring, boring.

"Thanks, Pete. I'll do that." He's right, though, about my mother; I am pretty demanding. So I think I'll keep my eye open for the book cart, and maybe they'll have more comics, so I can take the load off Ma.

The next day I see the book cart zipping down the hallway with a lovely candy-striper attached. Now here is a reason to look at books.

"Hey, I need a book," I call out to her.

She stops and comes in. She's about fourteen, eyes hard blue, framed with waves of red hair. When she moves, I can hear the swish of her starched striped apron.

"Can I help you?"

"Do you have any comics?" Dumb thing for me to say--all I can see on her cart is books.

"No, but I can bring in some for you if you like." *She's ready to go out of her way for me.*

"I'd like." *Is she giving me the eye too? Unbelievable.*

"Any particular comic book?"

"I really like adventure stuff. Superman, Captain Marvel, Green Hornet, Batman. Can you get me something on Tarzan? I'm getting hooked on him."

"Edgar Rice Burroughs?"

"Huh?"

"The author of the novel, *Tarzan of the Apes*." She reaches into her cart and pulls out a book. "I have one here. Would you like to try it out until I find you one of his comic versions?"

I'm beginning to feel like a dumb shit. I've read every comic this guy wrote and never noticed his name. Now she tells me it all came from a book.

"Forget the comic. I'd rather have the book." She hands it over to me. I try to touch one of her fingers but chicken out.

"Would you like me to come tomorrow and bring some comics?"

"Forget the comics and bring me all the Tarzan books you can find."

"Really?" She looks tickled.

"Really."

"OK, I'll see what's available." She leaves the room, her starched apron again making that swishing sound as she walks away. The clean smell of her remains.

* * * * * * *

A week later Dr. Hacksaw asks for permission to break the leg again. It isn't as straight as he thinks he can get it. Unbelievably, I have to go through the same thing again, but this time I have books and imagination on my side.

Nancy—she tells me her name is Nancy Drew--*why does that name sound familiar?* Nancy and my mother--I bug them both--have brought me books as fast as I can read them, *Tarzan the Apeman, The Beasts of Tarzan, Tarzan and the Jewels of Opar, Tarzan the Untamed, Tarzan the Terrible*–I can't get enough. Nancy says there are over twenty of them—I want them all. Me with the apes in the jungle, the protector of beasts. Me on the escarpment. Me in the desert. Me, Tarzan, the finder of the Lost Roman Empire.

Nancy, at my bedside, has just given me two new Tarzan books, *Tarzan and the City of Gold*, and *Tarzan and the Leopard Men*. I can't wait to get into them, but Nancy is reading me an article she found about Tarzan's wife, Jane Porter (later Jane Clayton, Lady Greystoke).

Jane, an American from Baltimore, Maryland, is the love interest and later the wife of Tarzan, and subsequently the mother of their son Korak. She develops over the course of the series from a conventional damsel in distress who must be rescued from various perils to a competent and capable adventuress in her own right, fully capable of defending herself and surviving on her own in the jungles of Africa.

Nancy says, "I'm an Edgar Rice Burroughs fan too. He's one of the first writers who brought women into the world of men. For example, he gave Jane the ability to survive and defend herself. He was the first to turn a super hero into a family man—protecting his son and all the jungle animals from man unkind. The first to put his wife on equal footing with men--and animals."

I really love watching her get all worked up. "What about Superman?" I say. "What about Batman? They all have girlfriends. Superman's Lois Lane, for example. She has a job. And then there's Batman's Julie Madison. Bruce Wayne even steps out of his super hero suit and gets engaged to her."

"They're all minor characters. The men are the heroes. They do it all, and get all the glory--not like Nancy Drew."

"Nancy Drew? Isn't that your name?"

"My real name is Kelly Drew, but my friends all call me Nancy."

"Why?"

"Didn't you ever hear of Nancy Drew?"

"I don't think so. Who is she?"

"Nancy Drew is a famous girl detective. There's a whole series of books about her. She's sixteen years old; her mother is dead, and her father is a busy lawyer. They have a housekeeper, but basically Nancy is on her own. Nobody tells her what to do. She even has her own car."

"She has a car?"

"And she solves all these mysteries, sometimes with her two girl cousins."

"A girl doing all that? A girl? Don't she have a boyfriend to help?"

"She doesn't need a boy to help. She can do things by herself. She has a boyfriend, Ned Nickerson, but he's just a minor character—like Batman's fiancée. All the girls I know love her books."

It's great to see Nancy/Kelly get all fired up about Nancy Drew, but I can't wait for her to leave so I can get to *Tarzan and the City of Gold*.

* * * * * * *

A month later, with my leg still itching in its cast, I hobble home. Comic books are dead--kid stuff. Now that I'm plugged into books; I'm Tarzan the Ape Man, the wordless man of words swinging from tree to tree, my hip cast blazing in the greenness.

1952 The Stage

August

Once home, getting up the stairs with crutches is a bitch so I get on my ass and bump up one step at a time. Earlier in the day Ma's cleared some of the beds out of the way so I can get through the living room. The huge cast around my leg is a pain in the ass, but it's soon to become intolerable with uninvited guests.

I ask Ma to set up my cot near the courtyard window. The light is good there for reading, and I can see what's going on below. I've read all of the Tarzan series, so I ask for something bigger— bigger ideas--something that will last.

The librarian gives Ma a copy of *Anthony Adverse*, Volume 1, and says, "There are 1224 pages in three volumes--I think this will be perfect."

I'm game, and I need the vocabulary. So I pull some nylon stocking material Ma gives me over the openings of my cast, prop my leg up, and start reading.

Anthony is exciting and easy to read.

> *This guy, who is a bastard son of an Italian girl named Maria and a guy named Dennis, while she happens to be married to a big Don, who don't like his wife being knocked up by this guy, so he puts a big sword in his gut, and ships his wife to a convent, and the sisters give the baby the name Anthony. Later when the kid grows up, he gets a job working for this rich guy who is really his grandpa—both don't realize it–then both do realize it. The guy grows up and finds his beautiful angel in*

the street—knocks her up and disappears to help save Grandpa's money. She don't know what to do so she makes it big as an opera singer and latches onto a guy named Napoleon, a bigger Don. It all ends up with Anthony and his little son on a ship heading for America to do it all over again.

A helluva story. It shows me that even a punk kid in Hell's Kitchen might make it. I like it so much I start reading it again. I balance it on my chest and keep reading until I lose the light.

The night sounds start to move in as tenants come home from work. Puerto Rican salsa, someone singing "O Sole Mio," the towering babble of Greek, Italian, and Gaelic bouncing from windows to wall, from wall to windows. Potsy's dad, the cop, beating up his wife again. Andy Corcus, the douche bag, wrestling trash cans down to the basement. Richie, next to me, sleepless, pounding his head on a pillow and humming himself to sleep and away from the noise.

A kickass hot night. Open windows, Sweaty leg itching like hell. I roll the nylon off, shove a coat hanger into the cast, and poke around. *Fuckin' bedbugs.*

"Johnny, Johnny. They're at it again." Acky jumps on my cast and leans out the window.

"What. What's up?" I was sleeping, dreaming of Eve. "Get off my leg, you asshole."

"The Kentucky girls are in front of the mirror, and their bras are off. Looka that. Jan is massaging her tits. Squeezing her nipples."

The sisters have a window directly across from us, both of them with huge tits and a lighted stage to present them.

"She wants us to do her."

"Get off my leg and get yourself some toilet paper. I don't want you coming all over my cast." I think about Eve. "Get me some too."

They massage. We massage. It's a good evening.

1952 On the Roof

August

It's a steamy morning. All the neighborhood windows are open, my leg is hot under the cast, and the itch is driving me crazy. Is the nylon garter I made keeping the bedbugs in or out? I roll down the nylon and jam a coat hanger down almost to the knee to get ahold of the little bastards-- it feels as good as a hand job.

"What's up, Johnny boy? Let's hit the roof. It's cooler outside," says Pidgy. "How about we go for a game of chess?" We've had a chess war for years. Some games last for days. Pidgy, reading my mind, is usually three jumps ahead. I have only a one-jump or two-jump mind, but sometimes I slip Pidge a few beers, and he gets fuzzy enough for me to take him. Pidge loves beer.

"OK," I say. "But you'll need to buy the beer. I'm fresh outta cash."

"Done." He swings the six-pack of Bud from behind his back. Pidgy always thinks ahead.

I hate using the crutches so I leave them behind and bump my ass up five flights of stairs backwards, one step at a time, my butt dodging around the occasional spit, dog turds and chewing gum, dragging my cast behind me, Pidgy following--heading for the big picture on the roof.

The Queen Mary is just pulling into Pier 17, three blocks west of us, its horn blowing and rattling the windows in the neighborhood. Almost everybody is outside shooting the bull. Off in the distance the skyscrapers do a belly dance in the heat waves.

* * * * * * *

Pidgy moves his queen, shoving my king into a squeeze.

"Did you read the book?"

"What book?" I say.

"The one I gave you, shithead. *Childhood's End*."

"Yeah."

"So?"

"So what?"

"It's my favorite book—the one that got me."

"Got you where?"

"Cut out that Abbot and Costello shit."

"Yeah, yeah, I read it. Starts off with these alien Overlords taking hold of the earth and kicking our ass for all the dumb shit we usually do."

"What did you think about the Overlords looking like devils?"

"Not much."

"Did you read it all?"

"Yeah. I read it all. A few kids become a super brain, then blow up the world with their power thinkers."

"They didn't blow up the world. Their minds turned into one new being and it replaced the planet earth with a super intelligence."

"The story is kinda hard to believe."

"It's not supposed to be realistic. This is science fiction, for Christ's sake."

"And there was no sex in it."

"Sex. What the fuck. This is science fiction—it's supposed to be about machines, time travel, other planets—you don't do sex in science fiction."

I'm starting to have some fun distracting him. He moves his queen without thinking.

"What was your favorite part of it?"

"The part where the super kids take over was OK."

"Are you going to make your move or not?"

"Yeah. What's the rush?" I move a rook and capture his bishop.

"Maybe you should read some other science fiction books." He moves a pawn.

"What do you recommend?"

"I think you should read *The Martian Chronicles* and Isaac Asimov's *Foundation Trilogy*. You said you wanted something big. The *Foundation* is a history of over 20,000 years into the future."

"Get them for me."

"Done. They're under your bed." He moves his queen. "I got you *The Adventures of Sherlock Holmes* too. You really need to read that--it's a classic."

I move my queen and say, "Checkmate."

"Bullshit," he says and moves his king. I guess I missed something. *Dumb ass.*

I can see him closing in on me. The hand on the chin is a dead giveaway for a super strategy.

I make a saving move, trying to put the squeeze on his queen, and open another beer to fuzz up his game.

Hand on chin—pinching his nose—scratching his head. "Checkmate," Pidgy says. "Another game?"

1952 Castaway

September

No moving air, bed bugs safe, lunching on my leg.

The doctor cuts the cast with his buzz saw and splits it apart. Nurse Big Tits screams, "Oh, my God."

Bedbugs, blinded by the light, their lunch box destroyed, run this way and that. Now I know what they mean by "crazy as a bedbug."

The doctor laughs. "I've seen this many times. Not to worry." He removes the final bandaging, yanks out the pin from my leg. A few drops of blood spurt out of the hole. There it is--a leg reborn—in the light—air blowing across it. Big Tits cleaning it with alcohol—feels so good. So free. Me walking straight to the girls. Me running, me flashing my new leg to the world.

"Hmm, it healed really well. What do you think?" says the Doc.

"Fuck, it's crookeder than before."

"Sorry, this is the best we could do."

1953 Integration

January

We're all in the hall milling around, waiting for the teach. I'm eyeing Eve. As usual, she gives me the sideways eye, and I don't do shit.

Meanwhile these two guys start giving me another kind of eye and working their mouths and fingering at me like they're gonna bang me around. Now Eve is beautiful, and I'm crazy about her, but these guys got my attention. George, the big one, outweighs me by fifty pounds and has a head like a huge coconut covered with steel wool. Marcus, the little fat one, has frizzy hair that stands straight up.

The show started with Mr. Higgins's English class, which everybody hates. It's all about this Shakespeare guy, who don't speak English too good. Every morning Mr. H. pours it on--spit dribbling down from the side of his mouth, drooling out words nobody listens to. Every once in a while an asshole student asks if they can read 'cause they think they know what's up. The old fart says no, 'cause he likes the flow of his own gusher. So it's no surprise we're always popping off spitballs and writing dumb shit on the blackboard.

Pissed off, Mr. Higgins hauls the problem makers, including me, to the vice principal--who don't do zip. So what's Mr. H. do? Well, guess what--he comes up with this "solution," and makes George the boss of our class. He's supposed to keep us all in line. Un-fucking-believable.

"Hey, white boy," says George, "Marcus here tells me you gonna kick my ass."

"Nah, I never said that. Marcus got it wrong."

Marcus says, "Nuh-uh, George. He called us both apes and told me he'd toss us up a tree, where we belong."

The part about the tree was true, but I didn't say it; another guy did. Maybe I laughed too hard. But if I called him a liar, I'd just get myself in deeper.

"I'll be waiting for your white ass out front after school," says George.

Eve is watching all this shit.

Now, this is one of those moments when you look for Daddy, or your big brother, or maybe the cavalry. But this isn't a movie, and I ain't John Wayne. So I use the back door.

* * * * * * *

I've had it. I'm gonna do something to fix George's ass. So I get me this fake stage pistol. It looks kinda phony since it don't have bullets in the chambers--or even holes. But I fix that with glue and some rivets off my motorcycle jacket.

In the hall the next day, waiting for class, George and Marcus step outta the line and make a move on me.

"The white boy is yellow," says Marcus. I look at his belly hanging over his belt and think of my fist in there and the vomit coming outta his poisonous mouth. By now the whole school knows how I chickened out yesterday--it's spreading like a disease, heading towards my guys on the block.

In my head George's face is in my face. I've got this speech ready on how I'm gonna climb through his window and slit his throat while he sleeps. Then if that don't work, I'll flash the dummy gun and see what happens.

* * * * * * *

In school the next day, Marcus says, "Knock the white cracker on his ass, George." Fatboy pushes him towards me. I look at George's closed fist; it looks like a bowling ball.

I pull up my T-shirt and show them the gun. They both back off. I put my hand on the handle. Fatboy's pulling at George. "Let's go. He's got a gun."

George is pissed now. He pulls away from Fatboy. Moves towards me.

I say, "You lay a hand on me, and I'll get you while you sleep and cut your balls off."

That stops him. He wants to keep his balls.

George says, "Later." They walk away, mumbling, making up new plans.

My heart is beating fast. I need a subject change. So I go off to La La Land, thinking of Eve, and me holding a ladder up to her window and I can see her legs coming down. Her hair is shining in the streetlight as she gets into my Cadillac. The trees go by with a whiz and we're into the forest--and my new cabin--and I think of what we'll do together by the fire.

1953 Automotive Shop

February

Ginzo says, "She keeps staring at you. Can't you see she has a crush?"

"Lay off."

Lots of broads are lined up across the hall from us, waiting for Home Ec to start. Some of them start giggling and looking at my leg. It's embarrassing.

Eve is in the middle of them, and I can't take my eyes offa her. The way she hold her books to her breasts. That little twirl of hair on her forehead. Fuck me, I'm outta control.

Me, Ginzo, and thirty other guys are shuffling around the door of the automotive workshop waiting for the bell and the Teach. We call him the Teach 'cause nobody can pronounce his real name. Besides, anyway he don't do no teaching. He's big on showing movies and rolling his ass around on a stool he made when he first started boring his students. Back to Eve.

I can't believe it. I even followed her home to see where she lived--Jesus Christ, what an asshole I am--what if she spotted me? Now she pushes her hair away from her eyes. Everything goes into slow motion.

Ginzo says, "I'll go over and warm her up for you."

"Knock it off." I grab him and hold him from crossing the hallway.

"Aw, come on. She's only a girl."

"Stop being a ball buster." I hold him hard. No way am I gonna let him go.

The bell goes off. I think she's looking at me as she goes through the door. 'Least I hope so. Ginzo points at her, then me, and gives her the "yes, yes" nod. She smiles.

Ginzo and me go to the back of the class for privacy. The Teach is putting the film roll on the projector and mumbling some shit about how this movie will teach us how to use tools. He finally gets it going and and asks some monkey-head to turn out the lights.

This class is great--love the smell of grease and metal. The workshop has eight tables loaded with everything from drill presses to ball peen hammers. All this stuff laying around and nobody using it. Story is that Teach turned in his retirement notice six months ago. Now he has a calendar on the wall and Xs out the days.

Primitive Pete, a cartoon cave boy, gives the class a laugh when he pounds his thumb with a hammer. Very funny, his thumb throbbing and him cursing. And guess what? The projector jams and the huge thumb dissolves into a burn hole. Muttering, Teach rolls his ass over to his film-patching tool and starts gluing the two ends together. He soon gets Pete back on the screen, making a lotta new mistakes so the God voice can look good, showing us what a dummy the cave kid is. Like the best way to hold a hammer and which way to turn a nut and not bang your knuckles. Jesus. We've seen this film fifty million times. Does he think we're stupid and didn't notice?

Ginzo says, "Eve sure is a great looker. Wouldn't you like to get your mitts on them tits? Hey, I'm a poet: 'Mitts on tits.' Get it?"

I give him the look.

"Jeeze. I was just kidding."

Primitive Pete's now into screwdrivers. The God voice gives the lowdown on how not to screw things up, and how hot shit he is, having all the answers. After we go through the rest of God's toolbox, the class's knocking itself out looking at the clock and bullshitting about the girls they'll never get.

Teach says, "Class, I have something special for you. I borrowed this film from a local high school."

Holy shit. Something new.

After the film roll--five, four, three, two, one--a pre-shrunk Primitive Pete jumps down into a carburetor heading for the engine's gut. Unbelievable. Getting on top of the piston after passing through a gas valve--that's a trick. Doused with gas, he waits for the spark.

Meanwhile the same God voice gives us a spiel on rings and valves and how stuff works. This shit goes on forever until the movie ends with the final spark and explosion and Primitive Pete popping outta the exhaust pipe, showing us how things come out. The movie ends with God's assistant, Walt Disney, telling us how he did all this for free so we wouldn't be fuckin' bored.

Not bad--maybe I need to bang around more in garages. I could be a mechanic--make me some big money. Would Eve like that? I could buy me a car--maybe a junker and fix it up. Fuck that. I could buy me a new one. She'd like that for sure. Maybe she'd let me hold her hand and not tell me to go screw myself.

1953 The Suit

June

I never had a suit before, so I didn't know how much damage one could do to my integrity.

Graduation Day, June 23rd 1953, at New York City's PS 17, is coming up next week. I've just finished my favorite breakfast–the usual when we receive the welfare check--a liverwurst sandwich on a poppy seed roll.

My father is sitting at the tub/kitchen table smearing mustard on his sandwich. He says, "We'll be going downtown to get you that suit this morning--not just any suit, but a very special suit." My graduation from junior high is special to him because I'm the oldest son, and the first one in the family to graduate from anything. He's never gone to school. He can't even read. He can barely sign his name.

After breakfast we walk up to Eighth Avenue and get into the subway. I'm always fascinated by tunneling through the belly of New York, moving in darkness one moment, rushing through light over the city the next.

We get off at Canal Street. Lots of small basement shops-- used merchandise and new hot items. The suit will be waiting there.

As we go from shop to shop, moving through street vendors, going up and down basement stairs, digging through the bowels of Canal Street, he greets the multi-national vendors in their various tongues. "*Bonjour, Monsieur,*" "*Bon giorno, Signore*" "*Buenos días, Señora.*" He's fluent in all these languages and talks constantly in all of them, chiseling away for a suitable price as he goes from store to store.

Pops loves to talk, but he loves making a deal even more.

Most of the day has gone by. Then we come to the basement store of Abraham Goldsmith, Haberdasher. There, in a crowd of dark suits, the sky blue suit lights up that corner of the basement. My old man goes directly to it, and the negotiating begins. He has to speak English since Yiddish is one language he doesn't know. This guy is fast-talking and tough. Round one: the Haberdasher spots my dad going directly to the suit and feels he has the old man against the ropes.

My father says, "A sky blue suit—what kid will wear a sky blue suit?"

The Haberdasher looks directly at me and says, "Sonny, this is a magic suit. It will make you stand out."

My old man smiles. He knows he's in the ring with a contender. The suit is incidental.

I think I'll help Pops out and say, "Isn't that suit a little bright?"

"That's right, Johnny—it will make you stand out." He starts fingering a nearby black suit. "This looks like the right size—put the jacket on, and let's see if it fits."

This goes on for a while—me putting on dark jackets that never fit—the Haberdasher trying to corner me with a measuring tape--and the old man fast-talking this guy into the ropes. Never mentioning costs.

In the 15th round the Haberdasher looks glassy-eyed and punchy.

Now my old man is ready for the final knockout blow. "Looks like we might find something here, but we have one final store to check before we make a decision." He points across the street at the Haberdasher's nearest competitor.

The Haberdasher, off the ropes now, says, "I'll tell you what—I know your son loves the sky blue suit. I'll make a special discount only for him. A once-in-a-lifetime transaction."

This is what the old man's been waiting for. "Let's try it on; see if it fits first." He waves off the Haberdasher and his tape with a toreador's swirl of the jacket and puts it on me.

I say, "The sleeves are a little long."

Dad says, "Scrunch up your shoulders—it should be fine."

* * * * * * *

Them in darkness, me on the stage, my sky blue suit in the spotlight, my leg a crooked claw. Everybody looking. *I'm fucked; my romance with Eve is over.*

Some asshole in a black suit goes on and on: "As we go forward to meet the challenges of high school--" "--always striving for excellence--" "--never giving up the search for truth--" I try to squirm behind some of the other boys. They shove me back in line--out into the light.

Finally the principal starts handing out the diplomas. There are over 30 in front of me, and the dark suits move in slow motion. "Richard Akrap, Maria Alioto, Don Allen--"

"--Maureen Flaherty, Allan Flanagan--" and then I'm next. "John Fleming." All eyes are on me in the sky blue suit. I grab the diploma, do my crabwalk off the stage, and make a dive for my seat. I graduate.

1953 Boxing

July

I'm at the Police Athletic League. Cops and kids all around me. In my corner Punchy's telling me to use the ropes--as if I don't already know.

Now I got me my chance.

Punchy gives me a shove and I'm out in center ring, acting like I know something. I do a lotta quick moves with my feet so nobody notices my fucked-up legs.

I start dancing around, jabbing at this red-headed kid, steering him against the ropes. His nose is bleeding, and his eyes are teary. I feel sorry for him. But I can't stop 'cause I'm winning.

A voice in the crowd says, "Throw in the towel. He's had it."

The referee pulls me away from Red. I keep dancing and throwing pawing jabs, crosses, and uppercuts, beating the shit outta my shadow. While doing, this I'm thinking about a week ago when I pissed in bed at camp. Fuckin' embarassing. They gave me a rubber sheet and told me that it was OK, that everybody did it, that it was some kinda fear shit tied to being away from home.

Bullshit, I don't piss in bed. No real guy does that. Next thing, they'll be calling me piss pants. A rubber sheet. Would you believe it?

Well, back to the ring. I hope the next guy's as easy as this one.

1953 Booze

July

Me and Pidgy are up on the roof playing chess, and the sky is mostly blue, but off to the east, over the skyscrapers, there's a buncha dark clouds moving in--grumbling and thundering. Maybe they ate too many beans.

Pidgy says, "My mom told me that she heard this voice up in the stairwell. 'Come a little closer. I have a drink for you.' She says, 'I keep hearing it say, "Just a li'l further up and I'll have this drinkie winkie fer ya."' Course, ma is inta booze big time, so she goes up further and sticks her head out over the rail and says, 'What you got there?' He says, 'I'm up here, Trixie. Stick yer head out a li'l further and you can see what I got.' Then he lets loose--right in her face--that motherfuckerincocksuckerinsonofabitch."

I say, "You mean he pissed in her face. No fuckin' way?"

Pidgy's so mad his pimples disappear into his red face.

"On your mom?" I don't wanna laugh, so I say, "Was she plowed?"

Dumb question. She's always plowed.

"Skinny the Blink?" I say.

"Course it is. Who else would do that?"

"We need to do something."

"Like what?"

"Chop off his dick."

"Stick him in a burlap bag with every kinda crap we can find and toss him in the river."

"Tell his old man his kid is queer and gives blowjobs to buy dope."

"Fuck his sister on a sand barge and bring Skinny the rubber."

"That's a good one," says Pidgy. "But leave out the rubber so she can get herself knocked up."

This shit goes on for a while until we burn out.

"Knock it off and make your move. I'll have you checkmated in the next two."

I look at the board and can't see what's for sure coming. I make a move anyway.

"Can't you get your ma to take the cure?" I know this is a bullshit question.

"Are you trying to distract me?"

He makes another move. I can't see where he's going. Maybe I feel a raindrop? I notice the storm is starting to slip outta the skyscrapers and roll down into the slums.

"I felt a raindrop."

"Stop stalling."

"Sounds like a bowling alley out there--maybe we better call it a day."

Pidgy says, "Make your move and die."

1953 The TV

November

Potsy lines us all up, his flabby finger pointing.

"You, you, and you." Pidgy, me, and Acky are the choice for the day, and Howdy Doody is the show. Googie, Lenny, and Ginzo are out.

Googie says, "Up yours, you fat creep, and stick Howdy Doody where the sun don't shine."

None of us really want to see Howdy Doody. The Robbin' Hoods real motive is The Lone Ranger. We're all fans of the Masked Man on the radio, but to see him now on his first TV appearance will be really something. Potsy's control knob has us by the balls.

Lenny says, "Howdy Doody is a fag. You gotta be a fag too."

Ginzo says, "Howdy Doody has a wooden pussy."

"I'll tell my dad what you said."

Potsy's father is a New York cop on the take, and his is the only family on the block with a TV. So Potsy, following his father's flat feet, leads us to the world's latest technology, strung along by a puppet named Howdy Doody.

Once we're marched into his father's apartment, filled with bribed goods, we see it there, in the corner, surrounded with boxes of new unopened things—the TV, all five inches of screen, the blue plastic fishbowl magnifier in front, the image a potential eight inches on a bubble. Wow!

Our plan is to maneuver the TV towards our hero, the Lone Ranger, but Potsy has his power hand on the knob for his beloved wooden puppet. He turns the knob; the screen fizzles and sparkles with static. Howdy Doody explodes on the screen, his freckled face blown up, distorted, and blue; his wooden legs and feet wiggle, clump, and dance on strings. We can see the shadows of the puppeteer's hands moving above, Buffalo Bob in his deerskin suit, leading the peanut gallery of kids into the show's theme song:

> *It's Howdy Doody time—It's Howdy Doody Time.*
> *Bob Smith and Howdy Do say Howdy Do to you.*
> *Let's give a Howdy cheer 'cause Howdy Do is here.*
> *It's time to start the show—so kids let's go.*

After a good dose of that, the Robbin' Hoods leave, and I return to my radio and the thundering hoofbeats of the great horse Silver.

It's obvious that the time has come for me to get my own TV.

* * * * * * *

Irv's Electronics is a junkyard--boxes of this and that, wires, cables, vacuum tubes, big TVs, tiny TVs, plastic TVs, wooden TVs. I've become a regular in his maze of technology.

Irv says, "Have you seen the Philco Predicta Holiday Model Swivel TV-Space Age yet?"

"No, do you have one?"

"Not yet. It's on the way." Irv always does that to me, tells me about some great TV and doesn't have it in yet.

"Take a look at the 1939 HMV 904 with a five-inch tube in the showcase; it's one of the first, made in England in 1939. Multi-band radio and five-inch TV. Neat." It looks like a wooden table model radio except for the five-inch circular screen and five tuning knobs.

"A little old, isn't it?" I don't want any damn old TV-radio, especially the first one ever made.

"Some day it will be worth a lot of money. The overall performance of the 904 is very good. The radio section is an excellent performer too. The CRT image is quite acceptable despite the relatively low bandwidth, primarily because on a five-inch CRT the lower resolution is not as noticeable--"

I have to put up with his tech-speak when he goes into one of his sales pitches.

"Finally, one cannot be unimpressed by the level that television technology had reached by 1939. Viewing programs on these sets is an experience not a great deal different from observing them on any black and white television today." I can see that he's shifting back to plain English.

"Did you get in the Bush 22 yet?"

"The Bush 9 with magnifier?"

"Huh?"

"The magnifier brings the image up to twenty-two inches—this one is especially interesting because it has a Bakelite housing."

"Bakelite?"

"Polyoxybenzylmethylenglycolanhydride, the first synthetic plastic."

He's starting to irritate me. "Do you have the Bush 22?"

"Over there." He points to a shelf.

"That's not twenty-two inches?"

"That's what the ad says—twenty-two with the magnifier. I guess they're measuring the wraparound effect."

"That's stretching it a bit. It looks more like twelve with the plastic lens. Why don't we measure it?"

"Good idea." He gets out a tape. "I'll be damned—you're right; it's only twelve. It didn't wrap around as much as I thought."

"Maybe it gets bigger when you stand back."

He scratches his head and stands back, looking for a change. "Nope—looks the same to me, twelve inches."

"Maybe the twenty-two is a model number?"

"You're probably right." Irv always agrees with me, never does the hard sell. Hell of a sales guy.

"How much?"

"For you, $130."

"The screen is pretty small. I was looking for something in the twenty-inch size, and I'm not too crazy about the plastic extendo-lens."

"Johnny, you've been coming here for over a year, and I know you're a buyer. How about a hundred bucks? I'll sell it at cost."

"It'll take me another six months to raise that much."

"How much do you have?"

"Let me see?" I put my finger on my chin like I'm thinking. "Maybe by the end of the week I'll have seventy bucks." I can't tell if he's smiling or frowning. Irv is a cool customer.

"Tell you what. I'll take the seventy and carry the other thirty for six months, no interest. That'll be about a buck twenty a week."

It takes me a while to run the numbers through my head.

"Done," I say. We shake hands.

* * * * * * *

The following day, after the elaborate opening of the box and the fanfare of installing the magnifier, and the rounding up of my family, I'm ready for the presentation. My audience, Pidgy, Richie, Charley, Acky, Ma and Dad, are all seated on the beds, waiting.

Ma says, "Do we need to turn off the lights?"

"No. This is a TV, not a movie."

"You saved the money to buy this?" says Dad.

"For over a year. All the money is legit. Changing bottles, washing car windows, selling shopping bags." My dad smiles. Pats me on the back. I think he's proud.

"Can we watch Howdy Doody?" says Charley.

"No. This TV don't get Howdy Doody."

"Will it make the electric bill higher?" says Ma.

"No. If it does, I'll pay the difference."

"Can we get Abbot and Costello?" asks Acky.

"We can get everything except Howdy Doody."

I'm getting tired of this. It's time to plug it in and turn it on.

I turn the knob.

Kaboom! A flash, sparks, the lights go out, and the room is full of smoke. My father says, "What the fuck."

Charley starts crying. Acky laughs.

"Goddammit," says Dad. "You blew the damn fuse. Now I'm gonna have to go down in the basement and put a penny behind the fuse. Shit."

* * * * * * *

"That TV you sold me was no good. It blew up when I turned it on."

"I checked it out before you left with it—it was fine," says Irv. "Did you drop it or something?"

I describe exactly what happened.

"Oh," he says. "What's your address?" I tell him.

"Aha, I thought so," he says. "The older buildings in that area all have DC current."

"DC?"

"Direct current. It's been replaced in most areas by AC--that's alternating current--but your home is in an old Con Edison area that still uses DC. That's what fried your TV. Tell you what I'll do. I'll send it back to the manufacturer for a replacement and give you another for a loaner, but you'll have to buy a converter for the next one. It'll cost you another thirty dollars."

"Shit."

1954 Epilepsy

April

"Hey, Bo. Your kid brother's having another one of his fits in in front of Sal's."

Sure enough, when I get there, Richie's squirming and jerking on the ground. One of the guys has stuck a jacket under his head and jammed a pencil between his teeth.

Jesus, half the block's hanging over him.

I say, "Pin his arms down so I can get the damn pencil out."

Ginzo and Hutty are wrestling with Richie's arms, trying to hold him down. I pull at the crunched pencil. It ain't easy 'cause his head is jerking so much.

"Hold him still. He's not breathing right. I need to see if there's wood in there. Who put a pencil in his mouth?"

"Not me," says Hutty, "I know better'n that."

"Not me," says Googie.

Shit. I'm supposed to watch him. What if he chokes and dies? Fuck. How does that artificial respiration shit work? Hands on chest and push--1,2,3, or is it 1, 2, 3, 4?

"God, he's strong for a little runt," says Ginzo.

"Is he choking?" says Hutty. "Looks a little blue--like he's gonna die."

"What happened?"

"We were playing stick ball and he just hit the deck like a sack of potatoes."

"Ah, it's nothing. Richie does this shit all the time," says Googie. "Just let him kick around for a while."

Skinny the Blink comes up and says, "What's happening?"

I say. "Hold onto his legs--I need him steady."

By now, the whole block is out their windows giving advice.

"Put a pencil in his mouth."

"Get his mother."

"Call an ambulance."

I try to get into his mouth, but he won't hold still.

Skinny says. "Is there wood in there? Remember the last time--he ate the pencil?"

Googie says, "Jump on his chest--maybe it'll pop out."

This is going on too long. Jesus, I wish he'd piss in his pants. Then I'd know it's over.

Some asshole says, "Maybe we shoulda called an ambulance. His face is kinda blue."

Old Lady Piper yells out her window, "Call an ambulance."

Richie opens his mouth and gives a big groan--I grab the pencil and dive in with my eyeballs. Nothing there.

Lenny says. "Should I take off his shoes?"

"What the fuck for?"

"My mother says you feel better with your shoes off." *Dumb fuck*.

I say, "Somebody hop that creep in the ass."

Richie's still bouncing around like Frankenstein getting fried. I hear an ambulance moving in.

Oh, shit. He's not wearing underwear and he's got a hole in his sock.

1954 Subway Initiation

August

It's a hot and muggy night. My brothers' wall-to-wall cots squeak as they shift and twist in the dark. Little Charley lets out a low hissing fart. Attracted by the moonlight, I lean out the window for some air. A light goes on in the Kentucky girls' apartment across the courtyard. I wait and wait, but nothing happens. Listening to the night noises of my brothers, I try to sleep and dream of Eve.

Three a.m., and I'm still up. The Puerto Ricans upstairs started a party at 12:00 and are still pumping it out: "Besame Mucho," "Cherry Pink and Apple Blossom White." Then salsas. Then mambos. Louder, then fading, then louder. Nobody cares. It's Saturday.

The naked Frenchman does his midnight run around the courtyard, mumbling some shit about his dead wife. Snyder, the super, charges out of the basement. "I'll kick the shit out of you, you crazy sonofabitch." Running in circles, chasing Frenchy, who's now slipping up the stairs, his white ass flashing in the moonlight. A door slams. "Next time it's the cops." Snyder heads back down into his hole, cursing.

The heat, the noise, and my worry about tomorrow keep me turning, rolling. Again I try to sleep. No luck.

* * * * * * *

A few days ago I followed Eve home. I'm not a stalker—It was just that she'd crawled up inside me and taken over. This is a long-distance thing. I've never talked to her, probably never will.

When I turn around the corner of 48th St. and almost step into the middle of their crap game, it's too late to back up. Moving off into the gutter, I keep going, hoping they won't notice me on their terrain.

Dingo cuts me off, his big chest blocking me. "What the fuck are you doing here?" I've seen Dingo before--pockmarked, his hair, black and slick, combed into a duck ass.

"Sorry, just passing through."

He smiles. "You're that Bo guy from 47th." He gets closer and in my face. Some of his gang break away from the game and bunch up around me. Things are getting a little scary.

"You're the creep that keeps following my cousin Eve, ain't you?" I don't like the word "creep."

"I don't know any Eve."

"Sure you do. You're following her around like a puppy dog."

"I'm just passing through—I don't want no trouble?" *I really put myself into a shithole. How dumb.*

A gorilla with buck teeth slides behind me, his arm around my neck. "Let's fuck him up a little."

"Lemme go." I elbow him and twist out of his grip. "I'm not looking for trouble."

"C'mon. Let's get back to the game. I'm on a roll," says another gorilla.

"It's your dice, Dingo. The game is getting cold," says Gorilla Three.

Dingo won't let it go. "You trying to fuck my cousin?"

Fuck her? I can't even talk to her.

"You're the shooter—are you in or out?" Gorilla Two says to Dingo.

"Yeah, yeah I'm in. Gimme the dice." He tosses a crumpled buck on the ground, unsure of what he wants more--my ass or the money.

"OK, got you covered for fifty cents," says Gorilla Two.

"Half a buck he don't," says Gorilla Three.

This is my opportunity to make myself invisible. I slither away as Dingo rolls the dice. I put distance between us, and the game goes on.

* * * * * * *

The Robbin' Hoods--me, Googie, Skinny the Blink, Acky, Pidgy, Ginzo, and Hutty--are having a summit meeting in our basement clubhouse. The agenda is me.

Skinny the Blink opens some bottles of Canada Dry ginger ale and slides them across the table. "Fresh off the truck."

"Ginger ale sucks," says Googie.

"You want Pepsi, place an order. I'll send out a cripple."

"How's your Momma?" says Googie.

"Lay off my mother?" says Skinny.

"I saw her going down the basement with Andy Corcus, and she never came up."

"Fuck you and your Momma too."

"I got me some donuts I picked up last week." Acky reaches into a bag and tosses them on the table. They clunk like cement. "Just soften them up a little with the pop." He shakes his bottle and sprays a donut. Everybody laughs.

"Let's call this meeting to order." Pidgy usually takes over because nobody else does.

"OK, Googie. Fill us in with your fuckin' lies," says Skinny.

Ignoring him, Googie says, "This buck teeth guy from the Dock Devils told me Bo is a punk. That we're all punks."

"This means war," says Acky.

"Total destruction," says Ginzo.

"Hold on. Nothing much happened to me," I say. "Just a little shoving."

"Fuck those pricks--remember when they hit Richie with a brick?" says Pidgy.

"Lemme get on with my story," says Googie.

"Go ahead, make up some more," says Skinny.

"So I thought it'd be a good idea for me to talk to Dingo about this and maybe team up?"

"Team up with the enemy?" says Acky.

"Join the Dock Devils?" says Hutty.

I ask, "Is it that girl again?"

"Mary has nothing to do with it," Googie says. His fantasy romance with this gang girl is the joke of the block.

"You following her home and lurking in corners. Doing stuff." It's rumored that he plays with himself in hallways while watching her.

"I never done any of that. That's a lot of made-up shit."

"What about all the love songs you wrote her?" He's stashed them wherever she hangs out. Everyone knows. Some of us have written love letters from him and planted them as a joke.

Googie laughs. "This is about us forming a new blended gang called the Ball Busters and us becoming the most powerful crew on the west side. Dingo wants to swallow us, but we're really gonna swallow him." Googie has a great imagination.

"Ball Busters. Crazy fuck," says Skinny.

"What's in it for you?" says Acky.

"Once we work ourselves in and break them up, we can run the show. I don't want anything out of this. Maybe a girl." I have to admire him. This is why we keep his crippled mind around.

"Asshole," says Pidgy.

"I seen you make up some mean shit, but this puts the cherry on the turd," says Skinny.

"That's exactly what Dingo said we'd do. Punk out."

"Who's punkin' out?" says Acky.

"Not me."

"I'm no punk. Anyway, this is all made up bullshit," says Skinny.

"Let's get down to business. What else did Dingo say?"

"I told him that we ain't punks. That Bo could beat the shit out of any of them," says Googie.

"Me?" *Maybe learning to box at camp was a bad idea.*

Googie says, "Dingo went on and on about our chickenshit gang. How you pissed in your pants. How you followed his cousin with your drooling dick."

"Lying fuck. Don't believe anything he says," says Skinny.

Pissed in my pants. Drooling dick. No matter who said this, the damage is done.

"All you have to do, Bo, is fight three little guys for five minutes."

"You're fuckin' nuts. They're all big."

"I already set it up. Eight o'clock at the subway stairs. They'll be waiting for us."

"You got me fighting three guys?" I want to knock him on his ass, but my reputation's on the line, and reputation is everything.

"Where are you going with this--are you going to punk out?"

"Are you calling me a punk?" I almost smack him.

"No, no. I didn't mean it that way." His paralyzed arm flops more than usual, and he hops back on his twisted leg and almost falls over. I don't know whether he's looking to get out of reach, or it's a brain thing.

"They said that, Bo—not me." He screws himself straight again. "They said you're a chickenshit punk. That you'd never show up. I told him he didn't know you. That you're the toughest guy on the block. You'd never punk out." Googie knows how to manipulate.

"Don't call me Bo."

"Sorry, Bo—I mean Johnny. "What'll I tell them?"

"I'll be there."

* * * * * * *

I'm on my way home and Googie latches onto my shoulder as I walk, hopping along with me.

"Get your arm offa me." I give him a shove. His body flutters like a bird with a broken wing. I laugh.

"I do the fighting and you get the girl. The bottom line sucks for me."

"I don't want anything out of this."

Aha. I get to run the show, and Googie gets nothing? Yeah, right.

"Eight o'clock down the subway stairs. They'll be waiting for us."

"Three big ones."

"Just five minutes. They'll have one of the girls clock it."

I really don't have a choice.

* * * * * * *

Richie starts pounding his head on the pillow and humming, his cot squeaking to the beat of his head. *There's no way I can handle three guys. Why didn't I ask more questions. How big are they? How fast? Will they stop at the clock? How important is my pride?*

* * * * * * *

Me and Googie wait at the bottom of the subway stairs. He's yakking about what a great opportunity this is for our gang. "Have you seen the girls? You can't have a real gang unless you have girls." All I can think about is my face and the huge fists coming at it from all directions.

"Here they come. Hi, Mary," says Googie. Six of them and a skinny pimple-faced girl come down the stairs. She has an alarm clock. I've seen Dingo before, but I didn't realize how big he is. They all look like giants. I wonder how far away the nearest hospital is.

"Let's go to it," says Dingo. Two of the biggest palookas behind him are doing lots of footwork and warming up. "Five minutes. No rabbit punches. No kicking if someone goes down."

I pull my leather gloves on with a snap and say, "Come on, you fucking punks. Get closer--I'll rip your heads off." Mary sets the clock. They back off for a moment, then start to work me on all sides. The clock is ticking.

I start by throwing single jabs and crosses before adding hooks and uppercuts, building up to throwing multiple punch combinations—all of which never land on anyone. But it keeps them back and away from my face. The clock is ticking. One minute seems like an hour.

One guy gets through my blocking with a wild swing that leaves him open for a right hook, knocking him back. Now I'm dangerous, so they keep trying to work behind me. The clock moves slowly.

I do some fancy footwork, bobbing, blocking, and slipping. I move a lot of air, trying to keep them in front. Once they get behind me, I'm done. Someone hits me in the face.

My enemy is the clock. Tick tock. Tick tock.

Two minutes gone by--maybe three--hopefully four.

I run up the stairs. And they all laugh. "Looka the punk running."

But I stop half-way up, as planned, and say, "Now I have the high ground–c'mon, you chickenshit pricks." They all hesitate, looking at each other, thinking who'll go up first. Tick tock. Tick tock.

Dingo laughs and charges up. I hit him with a half uppercut and put him to tumbling down the stairs. The bell goes off.

"Time's up," says Mary. "Bo's in--and Dingo's down and out."

* * * * * * *

The 48th St. clubhouse is in a basement storeroom not much different than our coal room, just a little bigger.

"Hi, gang," says Googie, his arm on my shoulder for balance as we make our entrance. Dingo and some of his palookas are sitting at a table playing cards. Mary is stretched out on an exhausted sofa, picking at something on her face. She pinches it off, studies it, and flicks it at Googie.

Googie, excited by her attention, thinking she's waving, waves back. "Hi, Mary." She ignores him and goes after another pimple. *This is the girl Googie wanted me to die for?*

"Hi, Bo. Are you ready to be sworn in?" says Dingo, ignoring Googie.

"Don't call me Bo."

"Whatever." He throws down his hand. "Full house boys, game over."

"I'm not interested in your crew. You can all jam your chickenshit gang up your ass."

"Hey, hey. He's just kidding. Johnny's a great kidder," says Googie.

There's a lot of silence. Everybody's waiting.

"You got a tick up your ass? What's the problem?" Dingo and his palookas get up.

"I quit. I proved I'm not a punk. That's all I wanted to do."

"You can't quit. You never got sworn in."

"I quit before I got sworn in."

"What about me?" says Googie.

"That's right. What about you? And get your clammy hook off my shoulder. Find yourself another crutch."

Part 4: The Stew

1955 The Hudson River

August

"Muh-he-kun-ne-tuk –The water that flows two ways"

The Hudson River is a mile wide between Hell's Kitchen and Weehawken, New Jersey. The river flows three hundred miles from the Adirondack Mountains to Lower New York Bay. The Hudson's two-way tidal flow scrubs New York's coastline four times a day—twice with fresh water from the Adirondacks, and twice with tidal sea water flowing upstream from New York's harbor and the Atlantic.

Further out beyond the pier's end, a swirling clump of flotsam—sheep's guts, pigs' ears, slaughterhouse droppings from a nearby meat packer—floats rapidly out to sea, passing Ellis Island and the Statue of Liberty.

> *Give me your tired, your poor,*
> *Your huddled masses yearning to breathe free,*
> *The wretched refuse of your teeming shore,*
> *Send these, the homeless, tempest-tost, to me.*

> "The New Colossus," by Emma Lazarus

In the center of the floating clump, a white eel (a sailor's used condom), some greasy turd balls, and a sightless pig's eye roll past her feet, and her balanced torch.

Me and Acky are on truck tubes. It's a hot sunny day, and the Hudson is dark and indecisive, running warm, then cold, as we move through it, heading for the pier's end and the current. Behind us, the Robbin' Hoods are diving and swimming off the dock; their voices get fainter as we paddle out into the unknown.

"My tube looks like it's losing air." I can hardly see New Jersey, and if I could—so what?

"Nah," says Acky. "It looks fine."

He's out in front, kicking and paddling like a duck. A loud, long blast of a ship's horn makes my insides vibrate.

"Looks like the Queen Mary's coming in. We better get moving," says Acky.

I know this is all a mistake, but I don't want to punk out. For months me and Acky have discussed the idea of crossing the Hudson River on inflated tire tubes. We know it's dangerous—once you get to the end of the pier the current often moves over twenty miles an hour—so the trick is to do it during the ebb tide when the Hudson is arguing with itself. But having the Mary come in at the same time is bad news.

As we clear the end of the dock, I can see her—she's three piers back and moving fast, her four 26-foot props chopping water. An army of huge tugboats is making way to her, blabbing with their tooting whistles and scratchy loudspeakers.

Acky, out in front, me following, kicking, splashing, is huffing to cut off the Queen Mary--five stories high, heading straight across our dinky tubes. I paddle frantically against the river's pull as it drags us toward the moving skyscraper. If we make it past the bow, can we make it past the 26-foot propellers at the stern?

I say, "I think we need to go back."

Acky says, "There's no going back—it's sink or swim." He's having fun. "C'mon."

"Once we get into the draw of the propeller—the show is over." I feel some warm stuff in my crotch–I think I'm pissing in my tube.

Acky's laughing. "Once the tugs take over, the props'll stop."

"Enough of this shit--it's moving too fast for us to clear it."

"Keep paddling. We're almost there." Acky tends to exaggerate. There's no way we can make it.

Now out of Juvy, my kid brother is a hardened criminal and fearless. He won't hesitate to dive off a catwalk higher than the deck of the Queen Mary. He stands out on the block for his ability to break into any building, jumping from roof to roof, inching along ledges, opening windows and doors to other doors. There isn't a movie on Times Square he can't get us into. We all wait in an alley at the back of the theatre, a door suddenly opens from the inside, Acky says, "Open sesame," and we all enter into the magical world of movies.

By now, Mary and her flotilla of tugboats have cut us off, and I see a bunch of limeys on deck, pointing and laughing at us, splashing through the guts and turds on our way to Europe.

I say, "Fuck this," and turn back towards the docks and calmer waters. Acky keeps paddling off into the white churn like the Lone Ranger, and I wonder if I'll ever see him again.

* * * * * * *

Back at Pier 88. I want to talk about a rescue mission for Acky. Nobody listens. The Robbin' Hoods are focusing on bubbles rising from the bottom of the river.

Ginzo says, "The dumb sonofabitch just jumped in and went straight down like a rock."

"Who?"

"Jimmy Jones," says Googie.

"No shit? Jimmy Jones?"

Googie says, "He comes up to us like he's some sort of hot shit, and says. "What are you punks up to?"

Googie goes off balance so he does his hop, twist and spin thing to get his gyroscope spinning right. He always does this when he's excited. He says, "Then I make some comment about his fear of water and that he has no balls. He says he ain't afraid of shit—I say he is."

Ginzo says, "Then the bully goes after Googie like he's gonna kick his butt. He says 'I'll twist your crippled ass.'"

Hutty says, "I told him, 'You and what fuckin' army? You ain't gonna mess with my buddy.'"

All this, of course, is said while JJ is under water and just bubbles.

Googie says, "I call him a rat punk." He probably said this while he was hiding behind Hutty. "So the asshole starts telling us how we should stay outta dark alleys 'cause you don't know what'll happen. So we're all pissed and start riding him, calling him a punk, and we keep repeating that shit over and over. Then JJ gets pissed and takes off his shirt and--and then his pants--and I see he has this big pecker with no balls and point that out--so we all laugh—then he grabs his crotch in both hands and jumps in."

"No shit, he really has no balls—I seen it for myself," says Ginzo.

"Pidgy says, "It's called retracted testicles--they're probably up there hidden in his groin out of fear and cold--they go in and out like a yo-yo. It's not that unusual." He pauses. "Shouldn't someone try to get him out?"

We all keep watching the bubbles and waiting. Suddenly JJ's head pops up, and he starts flopping around, grabbing at air, working his way to the pier, yelling "Help, help." Then with a gasp and a gurgle he goes down with the fishes again, leaving a trail of bubbles.

"Damn, that's a record—he can really hold his breath."

"They say that a guy goes up and down three times before he drowns."

"So he has one more dive," says Googie.

"How long can a guy hold his breath?"

"Five minutes?"

"Bullshit—nobody can hold their breath for five minutes."

"I know a guy who held his breath for half an hour."

Pidgy says, "That's doubtful, but if it's true, you'd surely get brain damage by then."

"That shouldn't be a problem for JJ," says Googie.

"The bubbles are getting closer to the dock—maybe he'll make it. Maybe he's walking on the bottom," says Ginzo.

Acky, huffing and puffing, climbs up on the pier--yeah, he chickened out too. "Who's down there?" he says.

"Jimmy Jones," says Pidgy.

"No shit?"

Googie says, "No shit."

"Somebody should get him out."

We all look at each other, waiting for a decision maker.

"Fuck the prick--let him drown," says Acky. He laughs. "Looka, the bubbles. Hey, they're stopping."

By now, things are getting serious. A couple of huge bubbles come up, and the water goes still.

Googie says, "I think he's had it–someone throw him a boulder."

More time goes by—seems like hours—no bubbles.

Pidgy says "We need to get him out—this is getting bad."

I look around–nobody's doing nothing. Still no bubbles.

Oh, what the fuck. I jump into the darkness and reach around looking for him. No bubbles—nothing. I don't even see my hand. Suddenly he's on me from behind—he's got me by the throat, choking me, pushing me down, using me to get to the surface. His grip is strong, and I can't get him off. So I kick and swim towards the bottom with him on my back and throat--to drown the fuck--and maybe me too.

Finally, he lets go and pushes himself away from me. At the surface I grab him from behind, and pull him, thrashing around like a dying fish, to the pier. The guys give me a hand hauling his rotten ass up onto the dock. As he lies there panting and spitting, I think of what he's done to us and about the monumental mistake I've made in saving this sonofabitch's miserable life.

1955-1959 Jobs

After I was suspended from high school in tenth grade--caught smoking in the bathroom--I didn't bother to go back. School seemed irrelevant. Ma and the old man were both drinking and then getting into arguments. I was old enough and big enough to stop them physically, but I couldn't stop the root causes. I decided to go to work. At least I could get the family off the humiliation of welfare.

My first job was delivering telegrams for Western Union. It didn't last all that long, but I learned about a lot of places in New York I'd never seen before. Like going up to the eighty-fifth floor of the Empire State Building or catching an old lady with her clothes off in a Park Avenue condo. But mostly, I remember the smells when the doors were opened--stale cigarettes and mold, armpits side by side with jasmine, lavender, and spaghetti sauce. I also learned that this job sucked and I didn't want to do it any more.

Over the next three years I had a bunch of dead-end jobs. One was putting meat into deli cases at the Food Fair. Here's where I learned layout and sales techniques. Beef here. Chicken there. End-cut pork chops, a cheap leader item, at the beginning. Best looking cuts on the bottom so you could move the older stuff first. I remember the boss had a bad leg and bitched me and the guys out when it hurt. When he limped, we knew we were in trouble.

We retaliated. I drew a crude picture of him and pinned it to the freezer door. Then we took turns throwing carving knives and cleavers at it.

Another job was working for the post office, sorting mail into boxes for each of the forty-eight states. I got to be pretty fast at it, but I didn't want to do that the rest of my life either.

I don't even remember the other jobs I had. None of them grabbed me. It wasn't till I started working at Hearst Publications as a stock boy that I had a steady job with dependable income. I don't know why they moved me up to a cost clerk. I'd always been terrible at math. I must have fed them a line of bullshit about my abilities. Oh, I could add and subtract all right, but when it came to multiplication and division I actually had to buy a book and teach myself the things I'd tuned out of all those years in math classes.

Once I had a good source of income at Hearst, I told the home relief lady to get fucked and drop us off the program. Soon after, the old man stopped drinking. I don't know if I embarrassed him by taking over his role as breadwinner and head of the family, or if maybe a doctor told him he'd die if he kept on drinking, but he quit cold turkey. He got a job as a night watchman and kept it till he died several years later, leaving me a 1909 silver dollar. Wish I had it now.

1955 Big Business

October

Me and Pidgy are on the roof of 525 playing chess. It's a clear day, except for one cloud sailing over us, slowly heading West to the Hudson River.

"Yeah, yeah, I heard it before--you wanna wear a suit and work on Wall Street."

"Make your move." Pidgy points at the chessboard. He's a little pissed. "Are you going to play or not?"

"Not." I'm stalling.

He smiles. We both know that he has me in the next two moves.

I say, "I'm getting tired of this chickenshit game."

Pidgy says, "Back to Wall Street. Once I work myself up in the business, I can become a stockbroker."

"Yeah, you a stockbroker and me a priest."

"This is the U.S. of A.--anything can happen." Pidgy looks downtown towards Wall Street.

I move my king, not letting it go, keeping a finger on it.

"Checkmate," says Pidgy.

I move the king back. Then I start drumming my fingers. I know he hates that.

"You always do that shit. Move, goddammit."

I know--but where the fuck to?

"After I make mine--I wanna go to Paris. I'll open this restaurant on the Champs Elysées near the Eiffel Tower."

"The Chomp what?"

"All those cool artists and writers walking by, sitting and talking art--Hemingway, F. Scott Fitzgerald--"

"Where are you getting the money for all this?" I say.

"The stock market, stupid. I'm gonna be a big wheel in high finance."

"You're a messenger, for Christ's sake--the highest you've been is the 65th floor of the Empire State Building."

"I went to the top once."

"You shoulda grabbed your bag of crappy ideas and jumped."

"Once I learn the ropes, I can make a lotta money in stocks."

Pidgy's good at sliding out of a fix, but I keep him in. "You're in France--can't speak French--got no money--"

"I was just thinking out loud."

"Thinking. How're you gonna get the restaurant--the dumb umbrellas--those French waiters that speak pidgin?"

"Lay off. I was just dreaming. Enough about me--what do you wanna do?"

"Well, since I'm delivering telegrams for Western Union, I got this idea that I'll be a big wheel in international communications."

Pidgy says, "I'm serious."

"I'll take up journalism. Then I'll buy a newspaper and make it international."

"I really mean it. France is where it's all happening."

The Queen Mary starts blasting her horn. Our guts and balls vibrate along with the windows below us. We go over to the roof's edge and watch the thousand-footer slipping out--her three tugs pushing and pulling, jump-starting her, and those who can afford it, on their journey to the Old World.

1956 The Block

July

It's over a hundred degrees; sweat will not evaporate. The nobodys and somebodys on the block are at their windows, or on fire escapes, or on the street below. Old Lady Piper's leaning out her window, her stool-pigeon eyes patrolling.

Me and the guys, too big to go under the pump, are cooling off on the usual stoop, doing the usual, but mostly sweating and waiting for the unusual.

"It's got nothing to do with size."

"That's not what my sister says; she tells me it's all about ball size."

"Why don't we go to Central Park and pick up some girls?"

"Jesus Christ, it's hot!"

Acky and Richie appear. Richie's holding a monkey wrench.

The girls, three of them, in penny loafers and stuffed brassieres, giggle and ogle Acky who has his shirt off.

"Isn't he cute?"

"Look at those chest muscles."

"Hey, Ack, can I do it this time?" says Richie.

"Nah, you're not strong enough. Pass me the wrench."

"C'mon. You said I could."

"I don't want you to have convulsions. Maybe tomorrow."

The girls keep looking at Acky. They nudge each other.

"Go ahead, speak to him."

"You go."

"No, you go."

Acky overhears this and starts flipping the wrench like a drum major. He's not interested in jail bait, but he loves the attention. The girls giggle and push one another towards him.

Acky's toadies come up to the stoop and strip off their shirts. Their sparrow chests are bone white. One of the guys has no belt, and his pants start slipping down. The girls laugh.

"Hey, Ack, you gonna turn on the pump?"

"Yeah," says No Belt, "Turn on the pump." He yanks up his pants. "Pleease."

"Yeah, yeah, in a minute." Acky is caught up with his monkey wrench show and the girls with the padded breasts. After a few more flips he's off to the hydrant, them following him like he was the Pied Piper.

Acky says, "Freddie, you go to Tenth. Artie, you go to Eleventh and lay chickie--keep an eye open for Jelly Belly."

"Do I hafta ?"

"Just do it."

Artie turns toward Eleventh Avenue. "Why do I always get the shit jobs."

"Can you whistle?" says Acky.

"Sure," says Artie." He's a new kid on the block. Dumb shit dressed up like Superman and dove outta his window. Thought he could fly. But that's another story.

"Gimme a whistle," says Acky.

Artie pulls his lips tight with his fingers and blows a lotta air but no sound. He blows again. No sound. He blows until his face gets red. No sound.

"Forget the whistle. Just yell 'Chickie' if you see any cops."

Acky twists the valve. It won't turn. He tries it again. The pump won't give. The girls start to laugh.

"Gimme the pipe."

"Got it," says No Belt, handing Acky a twelve-inch pipe." He inserts it into the wrench handle.

"This'll get the sonofabitch." It finally cracks open and the street is white water.

Now Acky props his knee under the gushing water, pushing, levering upward into a fine spray, Kids--jumping, dancing, wet, shining–darting in and out of the spray.

I watch Acky at the fire hydrant painting a water rainbow, his stream rolling down the gutter towards Artie and the Hudson River. No Belt's pants are half blown off, his white ass wet and shining.

Cop coming around the corner. "Cheez it--the cops." The kids scatter, yelling, "Fuzz, flatfoot," wet feet slapping on blacktop. Sergeant Jelly Belly runs to the hydrant—his gut flopping, wrench in hand. People cooling on the stoops, laughing, yelling, "Leave the damn thing on," "Don't fall on your ass, Jelly." Jelly Belly, sweating, tightens it hard with his forever wrench. "Goddam punks—lousy fucking neighborhood."

Ginzo comes up. "Hey, Bo, your little brother's fighting with Fatso."

"Again?" I run across the street.

Charley's crying as Fatso pounds on his face. How embarrassing. *Dumb shit. He's losing to Fatso.*

I say, "Stop crying." *This sucks.*

By now the whole block has moved in around the fight.

What to do? Option number one: I break up the fight and hop Fatso in his ass. Can't do that. Option number two: I egg Charley on, and he wears Fatso out, dancing around and crying while he's getting getting his face bashed in. Option number three: I stop the fight and call it the first round and give some coaching.

"OK," I say, jumping in between them and stopping the fight. "Let's call it the first round. Fatso, you in that corner, Charley over here."

"What you butting in for?" says Hutty.

"You wanna do a round with me?" *This may be Option number four.*

"I didn't mean nothing."

"Why don't you go over there and coach Fatso."

Ingenious. Fatso won't have a chance with Hutty as coach.

Now what? Charley don't fight for shit. He's crying like hell and swinging at air. Kids are laughing at him getting the shit knocked outta him.

I say, "Charley, you need to block and wait for a hole."

"What's that?" says Charley, wiping his bloody nose.

"Hold your right hand up to your chin like this for blocking punches."

"But I'm left-handed."

"Left hand is for leading and jabbing. Make sure you spread your legs like this. Bob your head--it'll distract him. Give him three jabs like this--then follow up with a right when you see an opening."

"What's an opening?"

"Just hit him on the button--right here," I point at my chin. "You wanna knock him out."

I know he don't have enough steam for that, but it sounds professional.

Acky comes up and butts in. "Grab him by the neck and put a thumb in his eye." Fatso looks around for an out.

I say, "That's not kosher--this is a boxing match."

"Fuck kosher--get a leg behind Fatty--once you get him down, use your elbow on his face. Go for his eyes."

Fatso pinches his knees together and grabs his balls. "I hafta go to the bathroom."

Acky says, "Better go home before you piss in your pants." He grabs Charley's arm and raises it. "The winner."

Charley's smiling now.

1956 Driver Education

September

Guys are crazy about cars, and I'm a good example of crazy.

"Sonny, this is a smoking deal. Looka that tire there. It's practically new." The salesman gives the tire a kick. "Solid."

"I was looking for a Ford."

"Can't compare a Packard to a Ford. Looka the seats. Plush. The girlies will love it."

"What about the Fords over there?"

"This 1949 Packard is a one-owner. Sat in the garage most of its life. An old lady owned it. Come over here and take a look at the speedometer--only fifty thousand miles."

"A Packard? I don't know--"

"You're a young guy. You hang on to this Packard Deluxe and it'll be worth a lotta money. They don't make these any more."

"But what's the price on the Ford over there?"

"I'll tell you what. I'll toss in another new tire. Fill up your tank. And cut the price a hundred dollars."

Now he's talking.

"Why did Packard stop making them? Did they close down?"

"They didn't close down. They merged with Studebaker. That's what big companies do."

I walk around the car and start kicking the tires like I know what I'm doing. "I'll tell you what. Toss in another new tire and we may have a deal."

"You're pushing it, kid."

I look across the street at another car dealership and say, "Lots of nice-looking Fords over there."

"You should be in the car business. You're taking me to the cleaners." He does some face and hand-on-chin shit like he's thinking real deep. "How's about me throwing in another tire--that'll give you new rubber all around."

I know we have a deal.

The guy caved in easy. Probably had it sitting on the lot for years. Who the hell wants a Packard? Looks pretty, though. Love that grill and the shape of it . I'll call her the Black Beauty. Can't wait to get Pidgy and the guys and take them for a ride. Maybe we'll be able to pick up some girls.

"This shift stick is kinda funny--can't get it in gear."

"You gotta put the clutch all the way down, or it'll keep grinding like that." The sales guy is laughing. *I need to get moving.*

"I thought it was fluid drive and you didn't need to use the clutch."

I'm bullshitting him. Of course I need to use the clutch. Finally I get it in gear after a lot of smashing and grinding. I pull out of the sales yard, lurching and bucking like a bronco. I'm finally in third, and it still wants to lurch and stall. I hear the sales guy yelling, "Gear down and give her the gas." I do that and--voila! I'm cruising for the first time in my own car. Fantastic. I push out the wing window and feel the wind on my face. Two blocks. Three blocks. Four blocks. Where's the radio knob? I look up and hit the brake. Too late. I slide into a car at the stop light. Wham!

Couldn't get to the brake in time. Jesus--four blocks and I'm already into a crash.

The guy is big. Gets out of the car and looks real pissed. "You dumb fucking kid. Don't you know how to drive?"

"Sorry, I was turning on my radio, and I didn't see you."

He looks at his rear bumper; then he checks out my front end. "Stupid kid. Get a horse." He looks at me for a while like he wants to kick my ass, then he gets into his car and drives away. I go through the bucking thing again and get the car to moving smoother. My heart is beating fast. *Should I try the radio again? Maybe it'll calm me down. Gotta keep my eye on the road.*

I'm cruising now. Got the radio on, and Chuck Berry is singing "Maybellene,"

> *Oh Maybellene, why can't you be true?*
> *You've started back doin' the things you used to do.*

Just the right song, so I step on it to keep the beat and get caught up in the music and even start singing.

> *As I was motivatin' over the hill*
> *I saw Maybellene in a Coup de Ville*

I feel the pulse of the engine and the music going down into my groin.

> *A Cadillac a-rollin' on the open road*
> *Nothin' will outrun my V8 Ford.*

I'm on the West Side overpass. The Hudson River. The ships below heading somewhere. I start thinking about Eve.

She's close to me now. Her head's on my shoulder, and I can smell the California beach in her hair. She puts her hand on my heart and and I know she feels it pumping, she then slides it down, and my legs stiffen. I can feel the throb of the engine and her hand. "I'll go anywhere with you. Do anything." I'm moving up. Moving out.

Some guy in a Ford drives up alongside me. I think he wants to race. "Asshole. Piece of shit." The Packard begins to shudder. I look into the rear view mirror.

What's that cloud of blue smoke?

1956 The Mechanic

October

"I hate to tell you this. You need a ring job, at least."

"No shit? Is that a big job?"

Mickey says, "We have several options. The first option: we drop the pan, remove the heads, and then unbolt each piston rod from the crank."

"All six?"

"Might as well."

"We push the first piston and rod out the top, replace rings, and put it back in. Then we do the same for all the pistons."

"Will that solve my problem?"

"For a while. But, you may still need to turn the crank and replace the bearings, and of course the cylinder could be galled."

"Galled?"

"The transfer of metal from the piston rings rubbing against the cylinder walls. Bad news for the engine block, which has to be smooth and tight against the rings. A good seat keeps the oil in the engine. Otherwise it goes out the tailpipe as smoke."

How could I be so dumb? This was all in Primitive Pete's film. One of the few classes I really liked in in junior high-- and what did I do? Where did it all go? *Jesus, what a dummy.*

Mickey goes on. "Option two might explain it better. We could turn the crankshaft down and polish it from under the car. If a cylinder wasn't galled, '10-Up' rings could be installed to increase compression and reduce smoking and oil burning without machining the cylinder."

"What does that do?"

"Using oversize rings on the pistons tightens up the cylinder walls so the oil can't sneak out. You'll be back on the road without the smoke."

"How much?"

"This option is a little more costly than number one, but we get a better look at the engine. Problem is--once I get into it, I may find something else that needs repair. In the long run it may cost you more. Can't make any promises."

"What's the best option? No Mickey Mouse shit."

"The third option, and definitely the best, is to pull the engine and do it right. A complete rebuild. Block, rings, crankshaft, bearings. The works."

"How much for that?"

"Two hundred and fifty bucks, and I could do it in two days."

Ouch.

"For the complete rebuild and installation?"

"Right."

 "Shit."

"Sorry, Johnny. There is a fourth option."

"What's that?"

"You junk out the car and start saving for a new one."

"Goofy's listening on the side. He laughs.

I say, "That's not an option."

Mickey's assistant mechanic--we call him Goofy because he prefers that to his real name, Godfrey--Goofy does all the shit work along with the mechanical stuff, and the guy is always on overload, running for parts, scrounging for the right tool, cleaning up, complaining, and when he has time, fixing cars. So guess what? They're always two or three weeks behind.

He could fix it in two days? Hah. He's got twelve cars out there waiting. *Now, how am I gonna approach this?*

I say, "I notice you have a lot of cars waiting outside. What about me helping you catch up?"

"Whaddya mean?"

I start walking around the shop, pointing at things.

"Look at that. Grease all over the floor. Some customer is gonna slip on it and you'll have a lawsuit." =

Mickey is starting to look pissed, but I keep pushing. "How about those tools over there--shouldn't they be cleaned and organized, make things more efficient around here? I notice Goofy spends a lot of time looking for things."

Mickey don't say nothing. I think I'm getting through.

I lead him to the bathroom and open the door. I pinch my nose. "God, it's explosive. If a customer ever goes in there, you'll never see him again." He don't bother to look. "I could make your life a lot easier."

"I can't afford to hire another person."

"I'll do it for free."

"Free?"

"Well, for trade. You let me use your shop and tools after hours to fix my car. Maybe give me a few tips on doing the rebuild."

"What do I get out of this trade?"

"I keep the shop clean. Floors, work areas, tools, bathroom. I chase the parts. I'm your flunky until my car is rolling. Your customers will be happy and you'll see more money coming in. It makes sense, don't it?"

He gives me this hand-on-the-chin look like he's thinking.

"No cash involved?"

"No cash involved."

He points to the bathroom. "There's a toilet brush in there. Get started."

1957 T-Shirts and Suits

January

The Hearst Building at 959 8th Avenue is six stories of cast stone. Commissioned by William Randolph Hearst and built in 1928, it was considered an architectural masterpiece. Above each entrance are statues representing the arts, science, and technology. Of course we never noticed any of this when I was working there. All we cared about was the inventory in the basement and the girls on the floors above.

Now a 46-story tower with a completely different design sits on top of the original structure. Completed in 2006, it was the first "green" high-rise office building in New York City. Recycled metal and glass construction on top of cast stone, an incongruous amalgamation of old and new technology.

In 1957 the stockroom, where I worked, shared the main floor with the mail room, and, together with the basement and sub-basement, contained all the materials necessary for operating Hearst Publications, from pencils and erasers to 200-lb. rolls of newsprint. There was also storage for back issues of the magazines: Cosmopolitan, Good Housekeeping, Harper's Bazaar, Esquire, Connoisseur, and many others. We were the guys in T-shirts. The men upstairs were the suits.

My co-worker Bob's a big guy, six feet something, a little on the fat side, with a chubby Irish face. Put a white beard on him, add thirty years, and he'd be a perfect Santa, cherub cheeks and all.

About a year back, he told me that when he first saw me he said to himself, "There's a nasty son of a bitch—I'll probably have to kick his ass and get him in line." Lucky for him--and me--we became friends.

****

It's Monday morning, and I'm struggling with an order.

Goddammit, why didn't I listen? What was all that shit about carrying? 642 divided into 97,506 equals what the hell—hello, I think I got it—1...5... Shit! the fucking pencil tip broke—cheap lead. Another pencil—do it all over again—stop pushing so hard—642 divided into 97,506 equals –lucky I wrote that down—1...5...1... and some other shit--damn, here comes someone—just before I got it.

She's the girl from *Good Housekeeping* upstairs, the one who looks like Kim Novak—she even has a husky voice. I can't take my eyes off her.

"I need a box of pencils and some scratch pads." She hands me an order form and I smell the forest and approaching sea. Damn, she's a good looking broad. Just like the *Cosmo* cover.

Bob's already seen her and is at her side. "Do you want them hard or soft?"

She smiles. "I like them hard."

"We have number one, two, and three—they get harder as you go up," I say.

She says, "Sorry--with pencils it's the other way around." The husky laugh again. I swear she must be Kim's daughter.

Bob is circling around her like a big puppy waiting--reaching--for me to give him the order.

"Are you related to Kim Novak?" I say.

"I get asked that a lot," she says. "A lot of guys seem to think it's original."

Bob looks like he wants to clamp on her leg and start humping away.

I'm getting the smell of her into me, and it's doing things. "Well, I'm not like these other guys." I look at Bob. "This is only a part time job for me—I'm really a writer, producer, and director." Bob keeps reaching, trying to grab the order form. He wants to take her down to the basement and show her his pencil.

She laughs again. More guys in the stockroom are moving in for a look-see—moving in for a move.

I continue, "You'd be perfect for a leading role in my latest film." Now she really laughs. I know she's onto me, but maybe she thinks I'm cute. I unroll my T-shirt sleeve and offer her one of two Luckies.

She looks at me and shakes her head. "No thanks," she says. "I've seen that movie."

Bob, pushing the crowd back, says, "You want me to place that order for you?" We ignore him.

"What kind of production are you working on?"

"Something about Hell's Kitchen."

"Interesting. Like the Bowery Boys?"

"I have an idea, but we'll have to get together and discuss it more."

"I don't know—I have a pretty busy schedule. Writers, producers, people of that sort." I keep getting the feeling she wants to laugh.

Bob grabs for the order. I pull it away.

"Tom," I say, "Can you fill Kim's order?"

"Yeah, sure." I hand it to him. She smiles at him, then walks away with this terrific hip sway, looking back at me. *Maybe I got something going.*

The crowd breaks up, dragging their dicks away.

I look over to Bob and give him that "gotcha" smirk; he gives me that "fuck you" finger and grins like the Cheshire Cat.

The rest of the day is numbers and puzzling long division. On the way home, I think about Kim's wit, and the other girls in my life. My fantasy romance with Eve is over. She got married and got fat. It's a good thing I never made my move. As for the rest of them, they swirl around in my head at night when I pole vault into bed. Not much there that's real.

1957 Lunchtime

April

Lunchtime is a great opportunity for us to mix with the other T-shirts and check out where the good food and girls are. Most of the suits go east for their three-martini lunches, so we rarely see this grander male species in the mix.

Enough about suits. Let's talk food and then maybe girls.

How about a hot submarine torpedo at Mario's for starters?

Inside Mario's Heroes, the smell of garlic and spaghetti sauce and newly baked bread wander out the door looking for noses.

"I'll take the sausage--lots of sauce," says Bob.

Mario scrapes out a handful of dough from a bread loaf then ladles two sausages and sauce into the boat.

"Coke? Pepsi?" he says.

Inga, one of the ballet girls from across the street, a big tall blonde, mostly legs, says, "Don't you love this place? It's like going to Italy." The line behind pushes her up against me. She smells faintly of sweat and perfume.

"I left Kansas to get this kind of experience," she says.

"Kansas?" I laugh. "How did you land here?" I imagine those long beautiful legs twirling and pirouetting out of Dorothy's house into the whirlwind.

"We came by bus from Topeka."

"Greyhound?"

"How did you know?"

"What's your plan after the ballet school?"

"The Bolshoi. It's been my dream since I was three. I'm really good, you know."

"Nothing should stop us from our dreams." I wonder if she can sing?

"What about you?"

"I plan to win the Nobel Prize for Literature."

"You're a writer?"

Boy, this broad is dumb. "That's right, I'm a script writer and film producer, and I just started working on a Chinese version of *The Wizard of Oz*.

"*The Wizard of Oz*?"

"Do you speak Chinese?"

"Chinese?"

"I have a part for a Good Witch, but she has to speak Chinese."

"Why Chinese?"

"The whole movie will take place in China, lots of midgets and short people."

"But I don't speak Chinese."

"We could hire millions of them. Just think of tall, beautiful you, waving your wand and their whole grey world changes to Technicolor and all them Commies--"

"I'd love to get involved, but I don't speak Chinese."

"Don't worry about it—you'll have very few lines."

"This sounds big. Do you have the money for all this?"

"Bob--over there in front of you--" I point at Bob."--the big guy with the sausage sandwich—his father is president of General Motors."

Bob, listening to all of this crap, gives her a "done deal" look.

"Hey, buddy, move along," says the palooka behind me. "My sausage is getting cold."

1957 Street Fighting

June

Skinny runs across the street yelling "Bo, Bo—JJ is beating the shit out of your brother." He points across the street. Jimmy is slapping Acky across the face—then he starts punching and knocks him against a garbage can. Running towards them, I can see the blood and tears on my brother's face. Acky keeps getting up. He won't quit.

JJ sees me coming and smiles. This is what it's all about—me and him. He can't stand it that I saved his life in the river and showed him up for the punk he is. I can't give you the details of the fight, but I do remember connecting my hard right, the snap of his chin and and the jolt to my shoulder, and him wobbling to a final thud on the ground. And me there thinking there really is a god, shining his spotlight on this sonofabitch at my feet.

* * * * * * *

A year later Jimmy Jones walks into The Bucket of Blood and asks me to step outside.

I say, "What for?"

"Just do it." Popping his fist into an open hand. Leather gloves on for ripping skin.

I finish my beer. "OK. Let's do it."

We dance around and jab for a while, both looking for an opening. He's better than before. I realize he must have been practicing for this—bobbing, weaving, and cutting. He's slapping me silly. Unlike the last fight, he's winning this one.

This goes on and on. Me dancing around, throwing punches and not connecting. Him bobbing and weaving and connecting . My arms are getting heavier with every missed punch. Finally, I decide to throw out the street rules and grab him in a chokehold, squeezing the pus out of his sadistic brain.

He grabs my balls and twists. The clock is on. It's either him or my balls. Is he gonna pass out? I squeeze as hard as I can. I hear a snap; he goes limp and collapses on the ground. He don't move.

Jesus, did I kill the bastard? Oh my god, a life in prison.

I go into the bar and order another beer. "You guys better pick up your buddy. The prick is dead out there."

As some of his buddies go out to see what's happened, I think about my future--iron bars, butt fucking, a whole new lifestyle.

Finishing my final beer, I go back outside to see the body.

They're lifting him off the concrete. He's coughing and sputtering. "I'll get you next time," he says, "maybe in a dark alley when you're not ready. That's a promise." It all comes out of his mouth with a funny kind of squeaking sound.

I laugh and say, "Any time, fuckface." I go back into the bar to celebrate my 18th birthday.

1957 Cruising
July

"What you going to call her?"

"Snatch."

I say, "That's too nasty."

"She don't need no name," says Ginzo.

"Pass the wax."

"How about Cunt Car."

"God, that's nastier. Add some wax there."

"How about Pussy Wagon."

"You're pissing me off. Wax the grille and shut the fuck up."

"When are we going?"

"Tomorrow."

"You got money for gas?"

"The tank is full."

"What if we pick something up?"

"I'll tell you what to do if that happens."

"Should we get dressed up?"

"Good idea. Wear a pair of pants."

Bob says, "I don't even have a tie."

"It's looking good. Put more wax on the hood."

"Should we brown bag it to save some money?"

"Great idea. When we pick them up, just flash your baloney sandwich."

"What happens when we meet up with three of them? There's only room for two."

"Keep waxing."

Googie comes into our scene.

"What's up?

"Waxing."

"No shit, you're waxing Victoria."

I say, "Where did you get that name?"

"Your car is a Crown Victoria, right?"

I say, "I like it. We'll call her Victoria."

Ginzo says, "Victoria. That doesn't say shit."

For those of you who don't know shit about cars and want to get educated, I'll leave it to you to look it up. Anyway it has a Continental kit on the tail, a Mercury grille, whitewall tires, a chrome ribbon that runs across the top and down the sides, separating a black and tan paint job. It's a beauty, that's for sure. Oh yeah, and a V8 Ford engine updated with Edelbrock aluminum heads and dual carbs. Split exhaust. Two pipes. Two Smitty glass packed warbling mufflers. A dial-down baffle to cut the noise for cop control. This baby would make your balls rattle and let the girls know you're coming. On second thought, I don't think you have to look it up.

End note. Two years later a drunk driver steered Victoria into a two-foot curb and gutted her bottom. Victoria was done, finished, headed for the junkyard. The cops felt sorry for the driver, slumped over the wheel and moaning about the loss of his beloved car, so they let him go. It was a long walk home.

Googie says, "The word's out that you're going to Coney Island looking for action?"

I say, "We're just polishing Victoria for a drag race in Brooklyn."

"Can't I come?"

A day later. It's a Coney Island weekend.

The sun is going down and the sunburned beach-floppers are prowling the streets now. Cotton candy, hot dogs on a stick, hamburgers, knishes, and corn on the cob. Lookers looking, pushing, shoving. The shooting gallery. The bang-bang-banging of 22s and the trinket wall with the huge teddy bear nobody wins.

The click-clack, click-clack of the roller coaster as it climbs and climbs .The long pause, then the deep breaths and hands gripping, then the vertical fall and the screams.

Uninterested, we drive on.

"Ladies and gentlemen. See the fat lady with three tits. Watch the crocodile man eat raw flesh."

"Three tits? Are they allowed to say that?" says Ginzo.

"Say what?"

"Tits."

Me and Bob laugh.

Bob says, "There's three of them. Pull over." I stop the car.

Ginzo says,"Looka the one eating that candy cane. God, would I like her to lick me."

The girls are giggling and grabbing each other by the arms. Can't figure whether they're pushing or pulling. One of them has this pink angora sweater and she gives me the eye.

"Look," says Ginzo. "She's giving me the eye."

Bob says, "No she's not. She's looking at me."

One of the other girls with a big nose and huge glasses pushes her towards us.

I say, "Then get out of the car and talk to her, Asshole."

Ginzo says, "I'm not moving. Look at the crowd-- everybody's looking at us."

Bob says, "Get the hell outta the way so I can get out." He rolls down the window.

I say, "You got a door--why don't you use it?"

The crowd is milling around us. Fucking up our chances.

"Who gets the crappy looking one?"

"Two of them are ughs."

I say, "I get the one with the sweater."

"Well, go ahead and wrap her up."

I say, "We need to cook up some strategy. We just can't pop up. What are we going to do for you guys?"

Ginzo says, "I'll take the one with the glasses."

Bob says, "Well, go ahead and make your move."

No one gets out of the car.

I'm pissed now. But not enough to do something. God, she looks beautiful. Her tits look like those fluffy pink snoballs. Yum, yum.

I open the door and get out. Maybe I can conjure up something original.

"Hello. How are you." Real original. Dumb fuck.

"Fine, thank you." She has this squeaky voice. A real turn off. Maybe we should leave.

She looks down and says, "What's wrong with your leg?"

I say, "Nothing wrong with my leg. What happened to your voice?" Arms reach out and she gets pulled into the crowd.

The guys are shocked at this turn of events.

"Bunch of dogs anyway," I say.

Yeah, bunch of dogs. But she sure has nice tits.

Bob says, "Let's cruise."

1958 Spaghetti

March

I'm having dinner at Bob's house in Brooklyn. His mother's big on doing great feeds—treats me like royalty because I eat everything she puts in front of me.

"Have some more stew, Johnny—put meat on your bones." She heaps more in my bowl out of a huge pot. "You're a growing boy."

"Come on, Mom. We're stuffed. Why do you always do this?"

Patty, Bob's girl, says, "I'll have more, Mrs. Boyce." Pleasing the pleaser.

Changing the subject, his mother's pot away in the kitchen, Bob says, "Wait'll you see Arlene. Great big dark eyes, long wavy hair, great bod. She has a really small waist. And real nice knock--"

"Bob--" says Patty. She's been trying to get me together with Arlene for a while.

"Top it all, she lives on Park Avenue. She must be rich."

"Bob, shut up," says Patty. "John, you need to know that she has a one-year-old."

"Is she married?"

"No, no. She's never been married."

"OK," I say. "Why don't we set up something for Saturday—maybe dinner."

Patty's the organized type. I know she'll get it up and running.

* * * * * * *

Saturday, 8 pm. A high-rise apartment house on Park Avenue. We can't get past the doorman to pick up Arlene. So he calls her on the intercom.

"You have a Patty, Bob, and John here." The doorman is suited up; he looks like an Air Force general, braid and all.

He does some mumbling on the phone. "Miss Milman asks you to please wait. She'll be right down."

So we wait. Five minutes, ten minutes-- Seems like an hour.

"This is bullshit," I say.

"Just wait a bit longer—she's always running a little late," says Patty. "It's what they do in this neighborhood."

"A little late?" says Bob. "It's been twenty-five minutes."

"Another five minutes, and we're gone." I've never waited more than half an hour for anyone.

Finally the grand moment occurs. The elevator doors open, and there she stands, a veritable Veronica Lake—my favorite femme fatale—the girl that drives me nuts on the silver screen—her long hair shining—an eye hiding—peeking through.

"Sorry I was late."

"Did you have trouble getting the stopper out of your perfume bottle?" says Bob.

"Maybe her penthouse door was jammed," I say.

"Enough of that," says Patty. "I'm hungry."

Getting into the car, Arlene says, "I don't like you."

"That's too bad—I'm madly in love with you."

"It's more likely you're in love with yourself."

"No, it's you I want. I'm mad for you."

Arlene says, "Are you always like this?"

"You remind me of Scarlett in *Gone with the Wind*. Did you read it?" Maybe the intellectual approach will work better.

"Your mating ritual is quite clumsy, and 'Frankly, my dear, I don't give a damn.'"

"Why is it beautiful girls are often such bitches?"

Her face is flushed, maybe angry. I think I'm getting to her. She goes silent and thinks for a while, then says, "Why don't we make amends and speed up our relationship. Bob, please step on the gas. John, would you kindly open the door and roll out."

Damn, she's smart.

"Looks like we've arrived," says Bob, pulling into Luigi's parking lot.

I say, "How did you figure that out, Sherlock Holmes?"

Patty says, "Just in time."

Luigi's is one of many basement restaurants spread throughout Manhattan. Red and white checkered tablecloths, lit candles in Chianti bottles dribbling wax. A painting of some Venetian poling his gondola through the past. Two lovers contemplating their future.

"What a romantic place. I love those Chianti bottles with candles," says Arlene.

After we're seated and have placed our orders and are looking at the painting, Arlene says, "I was in Venice once during my year abroad. It was very romantic—the music, the water's reflections, the seven-hundred-year-old palaces. I'll never forget it."

I say, "Did you know that many of the buildings in the canals are collapsing? That there are no sewer systems, and the canals have three feet of shit sludge at their bottom?"

"Doesn't it stink?" asks Bob.

"Only when the canals get low and the gondolas kick it up."

Bob laughs so hard his belly jiggles.

"Gross," says Patty. "Can't we change the subject?"

"You're a boor. How could you possibly look at that and think of that—that stuff?" says Arlene.

I've been called plenty of things, but "boor" is an original.

"That's a pretty classy word. Something you picked up on Park Avenue?"

"Let me define it for you. A boor is a crude and insensitive person, someone who practices rude and clumsy behaviors."

Holy shit, not only is she beautiful and brilliant—she talks like a dictionary.

Guido, the waiter, breaks up the action with the clink and clank of his job.

After we're served, I watch Arlene sucking a few strands of spaghetti, hesitantly, in stages; her tomato-red lips, touched by her tongue, glisten.

"Stop staring. You're embarrassing me." Arlene finishes the job, sucking and pushing the final strands in with her fingers. I think she really is embarrassed, but I know there's something new in the way she looks at me. The rest of the plate is eaten deliberately, rolling a small portion of spaghetti on her fork, positioning it with her table knife, and sneaking the bundle into her mouth--her mouth now closed—chewing gently. Her eyes on my eyes, watching. It's either a holy communion--or a mortal sin.

1958 Seduction

May

My brother Charley runs across the street towards me as I pull my car over to the curb. "Johnny, Johnny—how about you buy me a Pepsi?" His filthy face looks like it slid out of a coal pile.

"Can I have a quarter Johnny--can I?"

"You'll lose your teeth drinking that shit," I say. Arlene, my new love, is sitting beside me, my arm proudly around her as she snuggles closer. Some of Charley's urchin buddies cluster around, their dirty faces and hands smudging my new car. Paying no attention to Arlene, they ooh and ahh over the car as they run their greasy hands over my beauty's toned skin.

"Keep the mitts off, you little shits." I put the pedal down, and the engine roars them back.

"What's the make?" says Smudge One. "It looks like a Ford."

"What's with the Mercury grille? The car looks like a Ford," says Smudge Two.

"Can't you see it's a custom job—asshole?" says Smudge Three.

"OK—how about some jaw breakers for me and the guys?" Charley always sticks to the subject when it comes to soda or candy.

"Damn—you really don't want the rest of your teeth." He'd lost the front one in a fight.

"Who's the girl?" He finally notices.

"This is a friend of mine—her name is Arlene."

"Is that your little brother? He's cute."

Arlene drives me nuts with her long black, flowing hair—dark eyes–full lips–the kind of face you see on the front of *Cosmopolitan*.

Here I am sitting with this lovely, high-class, Park Avenue chick beside me in my two-toned 51 Ford Crown Victoria, and all I have for a sales pitch is the dirty mug of my little brother and his filthy coal-pile friends. I shoulda never come to the block.

I give Charley a quarter and start pulling away from the curb.

"Aren't we going to your apartment to meet your father and mother?"

I visualize her climbing over the cots in the living room and me getting her something to drink from the orange crate on the window sill.

"They're not home."

1958 The Birthday Present

June

As we head north along the Hudson River, Manhattan's towers of concrete gradually fade into the smog behind us. Now it's all water and trees and mountains, and small towns with funny names surrounded by wilderness–Dobbs Ferry—Sleepy Hollow—Peekskill—Catskill, and out in front of us Lake Tear of the Cloud, where the Hudson River was born and pours down the mountains and through the forest. It's as though I've traveled back in time, into the clean smell of the forest and the shining trees.

It's my 19th birthday. As we drive towards Arlene's family's vacation home on Lake Tear, she again promises to give me my gift in the mountain cabin. I can't wait.

1958 Union Square

July

Tick-tock, tick-tock. I'm under the four-foot pocket watch, waiting for Arlene, and I'm pissed. There's this guy nearby perched on a milk crate, talking about the end of the world, and he gives me the creeps.

"It's a beast with seven horns, and he is upon us--" He points at the crowd. "And all will burn in hell."

Fuck, I've been here half an hour and no sign of her. Got things to do. Can't wait around.

The guy on the crate is now reading from a book. "And fire will rain down on you, and the evil one will entice you into the fires of everlasting hell."

Maybe I'll hang around another fifteen minutes. Jesus, the clock is moving slow. Maybe she wants to make fun of me? Maybe she thinks I'm a joke. What am I worrying about—she'll be here any minute—I'm fucking cool. Tick-tock, tick-tock. The clock won't move, and I want to leave, but I can't.

A man pushes his handcart past me. I smell chestnuts and my mouth waters up. I want to go after him, but she won't find me if I move from the clock. He moves slowly away, taking the smell with him. "Chestnuts! Chestnuts! Hot, sweet chestnuts!"

Maybe I'll get the chestnuts and forget this bitch. No, I'll stand here a while longer. She did this before.

The hurrying crowd moves by me and the clock in waves—eyeing nobody—a blur of suits and dresses heading to do something--who knows what.

Alone on a box stands a man dressed up like the Statue of Liberty. The guy's face is painted green to match his green robe and torch, and his body moves like it needs to be oiled. "Give me your tired, your poor, your huddled masses yearning to breathe free, the wretched refuse of your teeming shore--" His voice gets muffled in the passing mob.

"What a lotta crap! I like the outfit, though--too bad he has nothing important to say," says a voice behind me."

I say, "You talking to me?" He's dressed in black and white, looks kinda weird.

"Just talking to myself. Got a light?" Irritated, I put a match to his cigar butt and smell garlic. I hate garlic, especially from the mouth of a penguin.

He says,"From NYU?"

"What's it to you?" *What the fuck is NYU?*

"Columbia?"

"Do I look like a spic?"

The Penguin laughs. "They're colleges."

"Yeah, so?"

"Sorry, I was just striking up a conversation."

"Take it over to the Statue of Liberty."

"Sorry," he says and walks off towards Liberty. I look for a wobble in his walk. There is none.

Tick-tock tick-tock.

I see an old dandelion in the grass and kill time pulling petals. She loves me--she loves me not--she loves me--she loves me not. Fucking petals are falling off--*I'll never know. Hey, hey, here she comes.* She's moving fast, waving. I watch her breasts bouncing, floating, as she runs to me, smiling.

1959 The Dickhead

February

It's 1:00 pm. Workers are returning from lunch. Mail machines start up; phones ring. The noise levels rise. Bob and I are filling orders from above.

"This is for you." Bob hands me the phone.

"Hearst Publications, stock room. Can I help you?"

"Are you the guy messing around with my girl?"

"Which one do you think is yours?"

"The one you've been fucking."

"Sorry buddy, but I fuck them all." I laugh. *This must be a joke.* "You'll have to be more specific."

Bob laughs, nods at me, wondering what's going on. I nod him away.

"Arlene," the guy says. "I'm Arlene's boyfriend."

"That's nice—what do you want me to do about it?"

"Stay away from her."

"Thanks for the tip. Fuck you very much." I hang up.

"What was that all about?" says Bob.

"It's that Dick that Arlene's been running around with."

"I told you there was something about her. Anyone that great-looking has to be fucked up."

"Knock it off. She's OK."

"Yeah, yeah, I'm just trying to help."

Back to work. Seven gross of number two pencils, two May 1943 *Cosmopolitans*, five reams of blue parchment. One dozen packets of foolscap note pads, 8 1/2 by 14. I can't make out that last item. Forget it–I'll ask Bob to find out.

"Bob, I got an order from Sophie in Magazine Design." I hand it to him.

"The brunette on the sixth?"

"Looks like."

"Yummy." He reads it. "Basement, sub-basement, basement. I'll need the key for the mags. What the hell is this last item?"

"You'll have to ask her when you deliver."

"You want me to go up?"

"I can't read that shit—you'll have to."

"God, is she gorgeous."

I made his day.

* * * * * * *

Friday--payday--suit, tie, hit-the-bar day. But guess what? It's an "everything-sucks" day.

It's 4:30, and the machines in the mailroom are off. The go-home mood moves in; papers shuffle, drawers open and close, eyes are on the ticking clock. The phone rings.

"Hearst Publications, stock room. Can I help you?"

"Yeah, you can help me, you prick."

I laugh at him. "Could you place that order tomorrow—we're closing down for the day." I hang up. This guy is starting to piss me off.

The phone rings again.

"Hearst Publications, stock room. Can I help you?"

"Arlene tells me that you wouldn't let her suck you off. Are you some kind of pussy?"

There is this long silence.

I know what he's up to–no way am I going to fall for this. But it's true.

Dick's laughing. "Arlene has been sucking my cock for years—what are you--one of those religious assholes?"

"Fuck you, you motherfuckerincocksuckinsonofabitch. I'll hunt you down and rip your balls off." My heart's beating fast—I know my face is red—I can feel the heat coming.

"Didn't you ever get a blow job, altar boy?"

More silence.

I say, "Where are you?"

He hangs up.

I'm angry—angry at her for telling him about our secret, pissed at him for taunting me with my own dick, disgusted with myself for losing control.

* * * * * * *

"You got a call," says Bob.

"Who is it?"

"It's Arlene. I think she's crying."

"Tell her to go away. I'm busy."

He says, "He'll get back to you."

"Hold on—gimme the fucking phone." I grab it. "Why did you say that to him?"

"I don't care about him. It's you I want?" She's crying.

It gets me right in the guts. *This is shit.*

"I have to get back to work."

"Don't fight over me."

"What's to fight over?"

"Be careful, darling."

"I have to get back to work."

She's still crying, and I need an Alka-Seltzer.

Then the phone rings again.

"I'm on my way over to Hearst Publications."

"Great—bring some pall bearers to carry your body away. I'll leave the door open."

****

It's 5:30. I'm waiting for Dickhead—so far he's a no-show. I'm pacing back and forth. I left the front door open---need to get him down to the sub basement—too bad Bob's not here—could use him for steering.

The phone rings.

"I'm waiting for you, you cocksucker. What's holding you up?" I say.

"Whoa, there, buddy. It's me," says Bob. "Why are you still at work? We were supposed to go out."

"It's that fuck again. I can't believe she would tell him that?"

"What?"

"Nothing."

"I'll be right there—don't answer the phone any more."

****

Bob's back. He hangs around, trying to find out what's up. I pace back and forth.

"I need you to steer Dickhead down to the basement when he comes."

"Sure. But--"

"Listen to me. Just steer him. Make it the sub-basement—closer to hell. I'll be waiting."

"What the fuck?"

I give him that "shut up" look.

* * * * * * *

Six-thirty. Dickhead is still a no show. I pace--mumbling, cursing, waiting.

"Look—the Christian Brothers did the same thing to me," says Bob. "Brother Sebastian told us that each hand job was a spear thrust into the heart of Jesus."

What would God really think about me getting a blow job?

Bob's digging. "Do you know anything about her family? You know she has a baby—did you ever see it?" He's starting to get to me. No, I don't know shit about her—what school she went to–if she ever had a job.

Bob keeps digging. "Did you ever meet her family—have dinner with them?" Me and Bob are great buddies, and I usually let him get away with a lotta shit—but when it comes to Arlene, it's probably a good idea for him to keep off.

I want to tell him to shut the fuck up—but he's right. I know nothing about her except the feel and smell of her, and me and her moving through the crowds, and the crowds looking at her—at us.

And there's the dark something in her that I want to brighten.

1959 Ambivalence

March

I try to push her head down towards my crotch. "Please?" I say. She did it for him—why not me?

"No I can't—I can't—I love you but I can't."

I try to move her face down again. "Prove you love me," I can feel the heat rising.

"No—you'll hate me."

"If you do it, I'll love you even more." *How could she do it to him and not me?*

"No, you won't."

"Yes, I will. Please—I never had it done to me—please."

"If I do it, you'll be disgusted with me."

"I swear to God, I won't. I'll just love you even more."

Fuck you, Jesus—I need this.

1959 Dropped

June

The newsprint rolls are about three feet in diameter and two feet high, each weighing over two hundred pounds. Once a month, we slip, slide, roll, and lower thirty of these from the truck to the street. From a flat at ground level we roll them into a huge loading elevator, take them down to the sub-basement. Once there, we restack them, like Egyptian slaves building a pyramid—one roll at a time—no machines—just muscles, leverage, and some linear momentum. Flipping, flopping, and sliding, we build four levels of them, eight feet high.

Out of the cave into the early morning sun. Unloading is our opportunity time. We don't care about the suits gathering, laughing at our T-shirts and sweat, but the girls—their upstairs handmaidens—that's something else.

Bob jumps on the truck and starts to slide one of the rolls off a stack. "Hey, Tom, get off your duff. Lend a hand here."

Tom's not much in the muscle department. Bob and me, for instance, bought a set of barbells and spent hours in the sub-basement working out. Myself, I got me up to a 200-pound jerk. Bob showed me up by curling the 200. Well, anyway, we had this idea to put on a show for some of the upstairs girls. Tom was into that, so he pitched in with the marketing and talking it up. He even did some weights for a day and quit after busting his balls with a puny 100 pounds.

Well the event never happened because none of the girls showed up. I guess they weren't into muscles like we were.

Well, back to the truck.

"Easy now, don't drop it on my toes," says Bob.

"Ugghh, this is heavy. Hold it, hold it," says Tom. "It's starting to slip. I don't know if I can hold it." He jumps away. Bang. The roll hits the deck flat, and the truck shudders.

Bob looks at his feet to see if he still has them. "Get the fuck offa here. You almost crushed my toes."

"I'm sorry, Bob. It slipped."

"John, gimme a hand. Tom, you take a break--before you kill someone."

Lucky for Tom he has his mom's house for our parties. He sure isn't worth a shit on the job.

1959 The Goombahs

July

A month ago Bob offered to take me to a bar in Brooklyn. "Lots of action," he said. He told me there was something special about the place, then gave me this twisty laugh and said, "Wait'll you see the girls."

What the hell – why not? It's Friday. "Do I need a suit?"

"Nah, it's just a working place."

In the subway an old woman yawns, I yawn. The yawn creeps slowly down the car, zigging and zagging across the aisle like a virus. WALL STREET. Doors open. Fifty waiting grey flannel suits squeeze in, snatching straps and picking up the yawn. But not Bob--he keeps talking about his neighborhood, his women, his conquests, big talk rattling and bumping along as the subway rushes towards Flatbush. Diana with the hard nipples, Susie with the quivering legs, Mary, the virgin with fast feet he never caught, Flatbush this and Flatbush that, where beer and broads meld and no one ever yawns. FLATBUSH AVENUE.

* * * * * *

"What the hell kinda a bar is this? Where's the girls?" I look around at the bar and then the tables. They all look like Wops. Two bald guys twisting spaghetti on forks and speaking Italian, their bibs splattered with sauce. The rest of the tables are empty. Bob leads me over to the bibs. Some huge guy steps outta the shadow.

"Yo, Frank. It's me, Bob," He puts his hands up to get Frankenstein to back off. "How's things, Tony?

"How ya doin', kid?" The Bib nods the Shadow back into the darkness.

"My Ma wants me to thank you for that thing you did for her."

"Fageddaboudit. Who's the friend?"

"This is Johnny—he's OK."

"Where you from, kid?"

"Tenth Avenue and Forty-seventh Street."

"Hell's Kitchen?"

"Right."

"I used to live there on Forty-eighth. Is Old Lady Piper still there?"

"Yeah, she's still there, perched on her window sill like a stool pigeon."

"Ya know John Abruzzi on Forty-seventh?"

"The ice man?"

"Yeah, he had a stroke carrying ice up to the sixth floor in 525."

"That's my building."

"No shit. Lots of micks in that building."

"Johnny is part Italian on his old man's side" says Bob.

"No shit. Two goombahs that look like micks," says Tony, laughing.

Tony points his fork at us and then at the bar. Bored with the conversation, he sticks his fork into his spaghetti. Then he starts blabbing in Italian, hands and fork flying, making pointless points. The bib guy keeps nodding up and down like Tony has something to say.

Following instructions, we go to the bar with the lowgrades—three are wearing porkpie hats and sharkskin suits–a dead giveaway.

We have a few beers, and I look up at this sign. NO WOMEN ALLOWED.

"What the fuck is that?"

Bob laughs, "I told you it was something special."

"Why do you always do this shit?"

"For the adventure. It's sorta like cruising down the Amazon River–you don't know what's going to eat you."

Not wanting to get eaten, I wonder how to get out of this place.

"Pop, pop, pop."

"What's with the popping shit coming outta the floor?"

Bob laughs. "Target practice."

"Huh?"

"They have a target range in the basement."

"All right, let's get outta here." I start towards the door.

"Hold it a min--Tony's sending Frank over."

"Thump-thump-thump." Frankenstein's size twenty-four, inch-high shoes thump the floor.

"The boss says--duh, you wanna break some legs?"

Bob laughs and says, "Whose legs get the breaking? Ours?"

"Dunno. Let me check."

"Thump-thump-thump." Back he goes to the boss. The boss laughs and calls another guy with smaller feet and maybe a bigger brain.

"Let's get the fuck outta here," I say.

The Brain comes over. He's laughing too. "Tony just wants Frank to bring you back for a little talk on some business."

"Business?" says Bob.

"Business?" I say.

"Tony wants to talk." He makes a motion with his hand. It might as well've been Frankenstein's foot.

"I got a proposition for you guys," Tony says.

"Sure, Tony. What can we do for you?" says Bob.

"I got this mick who's in arrears."

"Yeah, Tony?"

"Maybe you guys are interested in a little money?"

I can't take my eyes off Frankenstein's shoes. I see my head as a huge splotch of blood and bone and his foot coming down for the final smear.

"Maybe some girls." Tony looks at our clothes and laughs. "Maybe some new rags?"

"Sure," said Bob. "Clothes, girls--whatever you say, Tony."

I start to say something. Bob gives me the "shut up" look.

"I got this mick deadbeat that needs his knees capped—you guys interested?"

"Bob says "Can we think about that?" He looks at me and whispers, "Isn't this fun?"

"Sure, kid. Let Ernie know. It's gotta be done this week."

If this was a movie, I wouldn't believe it.

Of course we never go back to see Tony. Last I heard, he had his face and brains spread out in his spaghetti plate—what a sauce. Lucky for him he had his bib on.

1959 Dumped

August

Late summer and Central Park is blooming with dandelions and daisies. The dark lake reflects the nearby buildings on Park Avenue, where she lives.

"I'm sorry, but we can't go on this way," Arlene says.

"What do you mean?"

"There's no easy way to say this--we have to break up."

I'm stunned.

"We can't go on like this."

"Like what?"

"It's hard to explain. Why don't we just end it?"

Long silence. "It's Dickhead, isn't it?"

"No, it's not just him."

I look at her eyes, her mouth, and the shape of her and don't want it to end. But then I see myself standing in this field of flowers, ready to cry.

How do I come out cool in this situation?

I pick up this daisy and say, "I could pull off the petals and see if you really love me, but it's a weed and would probably lie."

I walk away, kicking and stomping on every fuckin' daisy in my path.

1959 The Enigma

December

Daddy collapsed on Broadway. Everybody was there, but nobody was there. For over an hour, his body lay on the sidewalk--trash, something to be avoided by shoes--and eyes.

A knock at the door. Officer Flanagan's standing there, his hat in his hands.

My old man was an enigma. He had no bank account, and when he died there was nothing left except two silver dollars for me and Acky. We knew very little about Pop. He hated that word, so we called him Daddy, and the guys kidded us: "Daddy, Daddy. Where is Mommy, Mommy?" And I'd kick their asses--or at least threaten to.

We knew he sang, made great pasta e fagioli, *that he drank hard liquor, but never at home, that he spoke five languages and couldn't read or write, that he was a painter, the kind with a big brush that paints house walls. We knew he had jumped over a six-foot wall when I was born. We knew that he had painted the Empire State Building outside on a scaffold, hopefully while sober. We knew that he had ridden the rails, that he had lived during the Depression, that he had built parks and roads for the WPA, that after all that he was jobless and drunk most of the time. We knew that he had sailed around the world as a merchant marine. We knew that he didn't talk about himself, that he propped chairs against our steel-clad door to keep someone out. We knew his Italian friends, who became our godparents, and there was something sacred and secret about them.*

We never looked back much then. History, like the news, was unimportant—getting the booze, the check, paying the rent, buying food, shirts, and shoes obsessed us. Wars and world news were irrelevant.

Today, nineteen years older than my dad when he died, I now know that my father was born in New York City in 1902 to John Fleming of Dublin, Ireland and Maria Cavallo of Bordeaux, France. I know that my father married my mother on August 26, 1936 when he was thirty-four years old. I know that he lived the rest of his life with his family, drunk or sober. I know that he collapsed on some New York City street and died in the hospital on December 29, 1959. I know, because I saw it. I remember him leaving me and Acky two silver dollars, and him in a hole somewhere in New York's Potter's Field, three coffins down with two strangers on top of him. And no cross to guide him.

Thinking back, I made a lot of assumptions about my father, and I really didn't know shit about him.

Did he really jump over a six foot fence when I was born? I was probably in my mother's arms when he told her this story, so she didn't see it. What fence? Was he an Olympian or a drunk?

Why did it take three years for my parents to have me? How could a man live through the Depression, ride the rails, build parks with the WPA, sail around the world, and not have a story to tell to his children? Why would he prop chairs against our door and sing opera? Why would some woman at his funeral tell me that our last name was Ferrari, not Fleming? Maybe he did tell us these and many stories and I wasn't listening because I lost respect for him. Maybe he didn't tell us his story because he sensed that and had no respect for himself. Maybe now I know more than I knew. Maybe.

Who is the enigma? Daddy? My father? The old man? Or is it me?

1959 Unrequited

December

Why the hell did she call me? It's been over four months. I slip on the ice and fall on my dick. I have a hard time getting up. *Why does she wanna meet me in the park? It's colder than a well digger's ass. Where the fuck did I get that? Never seen a well or a fuckin' digger.* Lots of Christmas shit still hanging up.

Fuck her. Yeah, that's what I wanna do--fuck her.

She's out on the ice and snow, and there ain't no daisies in Central Park.

Arlene says, "I have something to tell you."

"Okaaay."

I don't want to hurt you, but--"

I hate that word "but." Whenever someone gives me the *but,* I know some shit is coming down.

"I'm pregnant," she says.

"What's that got to do with me?"

"I'm sorry I left you." I don't see any belly there. Or maybe I do.

"You're the only one. I love you."

God, she's gorgeous. It looks like she's gonna cry.

"What happened to the dickhead?"

"I realized he wasn't the one for me." *How dumb does she think I am?*

"How does it feel to get dumped?"

"I'm sorry."

Goddammit, she's crying. Something's crawling in my belly. *I'm getting sick. I need to leave.*

I say, "Did you tell your parents?"

Now she really starts crying. *Who's she crying about--her parents, him, or me?*

"No, I couldn't until I spoke to you."

Here it comes. Which finger--the pointer or the middle?

"Why me? What about that dickhead that put you in this situation?"

"It's more complicated than that."

"You've been away for four months. I almost forgot about you."

Now she really starts crying. She looks so small there in the cold, and I want to hold her, but I keep my hands in my pockets for protection.

1960 Saying Goodbye

January

Bob says, "What the hell would you go to Minnesota for? Nothing up there but cold, snow, and squareheads. For chrissakes, they don't even speak English."

"I'm moving the family—there's trees, lakes, wolves."

"Move to Brooklyn. We got all of that."

"It's all the same shit. I need to get my mom out and away from the booze. Since my old man croaked, we got nothing keeping us here. My brothers are turning into gangsters."

"That sounds like a bunch of phony excuses. What's really bothering you?"

"Well, Arlene's back." I had to tell somebody.

"That bitch that dumped you?"

"She says she's pregnant."

"No shit? Is she accusing you?"

"Not really."

"But she's been gone for—what is it? Four months?"

"Almost five."

"Well, if it happened five months ago you should be able to see something. Did you?"

"She's as flat as ever." I know all this shit—nine months to have a baby—four or five months for it to show.

"Then what are you worried about?"

"I'm not worried."

"You're thinking of moving your whole family to Minnesota and you say you're not worried."

Sure I'm worried—worried that Dick knocked her up—worried that I knocked her up—worried that I'll lose her–worried that I'll keep her.

"Let's lay off it for a while. I'm not feeling too good."

"Sure, Johnny. I'm just trying to help."

"Let's get back to work. Here's an order for marketing–some pencils and other shit."

"I'll tell you what. Let's go over to my house this evening. You can have dinner with us and maybe you'll forget all this crap for a while."

"I can't. I have something to do." Yeah—lay in bed thinking about her.

"My mom's having corned beef and cabbage."

"OK." I hand him the order.

"She asked especially for you to come. Corned beef."

"I said OK."

1960 The Last Supper

January

"Pass the cabbage."

"Mustard, please."

"More corned beef, Johnny? Here, have a bigger portion. I love to have you over—you eat everything I put in front of you."

Bob's mom and three brothers eat all sitting at one table—would you believe it? Just like TV characters—silver forks, spoons, knives, a red flowered tablecloth--and napkins too, folded into neat triangles. A huge bowl of cabbage, mountains of corned beef, and of course steaming potatoes, mashed and unmashed. And to me the most unbelievable thing of all—homemade bread. Today's bake is a fragrant multigrain with a thick crust. Aromas of cooked cabbage, corned beef and fresh bread get me off the subject of Arlene.

Bob's mom is an interesting woman—four sons, each with a shadow father of his own. Bob is six feet two, a good looking guy with green eyes and a sunshine smile. Larry, the oldest, is short and stout, with brown eyes and a dark and fiery personality. The youngest, Chuck and Buddy--who knows about Chuck and Buddy? They never talk, except to one another in a special kind of twin language.

I once asked Bob about this strange salad mix. "Mom don't like men, but she loves bringing up kids."

That didn't tell me much, but I really didn't care.

I like the rawness of this family and have become part of it. Maybe that's why it's so hard to spring it on them that we're leaving for Minnesota.

"Pass the mustard. Wake up, Johnny. Pass the damn mustard," says Larry. "Are you dozing off?"

"Johnny's thinking about moving to Minnesota," says Bob.

"Dipshit idea." Larry reaches across the table and grabs the mustard.

"Watch your language at the table," says Bob's mom. "Are you really leaving, Johnny?"

"I'm thinking about it."

1960 Moving Out

January

I'm in bed, eyes crusty, hanging onto a dream of Minnesota woods and flashes of being there when I was nine years old. Wolves howling across the lake, a loon diving, disappearing into dark water, and the hissing trees and the smell of the pines.

I'm awake now. Charley and Richie are talking some shit about Skinny the Blink's brother stealing their chocolate milk.

Me, surrounded by kids and cots. The kitchen tub--the orange crate fridge with the always bad milk--the garbage--the roaches--the voices in the airshaft. My old man's death rattle. And the silver dollars he left me and Acky.

Arlene, her belly fucked up and maybe swelling.

I get up and go into the kitchen. Ma's doing one of her puzzles on the tub table.

I rub the crud off my eyes. The hairs on the back of my neck stand up. She's doing my dream.

"I need another sky." She pushes the pieces around. There's a lake surrounded by tall pines and birds and ducks, maybe even a loon.

"Ma? Where did you get that?"

"What?" She finds a blue piece, but it don't fit.

"The puzzle."

"At the Salvation Army. Why?"

"What do you think about moving to Minnesota?"

"You know I think about it all the time."

"Why don't we do it?"

All my life I've heard Ma talk about moving back to Minnesota.

"You really mean it?"

"I'm serious."

Ma says, "Can we afford it?"

"I got it all worked out. I have enough put away for six months. What about leaving the day after tomorrow?"

"The day after tomorrow--that's Wednesday? We'll be getting our Social Security check."

"Oh yeah. I forgot. I'll have to stick around till Friday for my paycheck."

"So we can leave on Saturday?"

"Yeah. Let whoever you want to know know. I'll need to talk to some people and get the car ready."

She gets up quickly from the table. "I'll need to do the laundry." She reaches under the sink for the scrub board. "Charley, take off those dirty pants. I'll need some boxes. Will we have enough room in the car?"

I say, "It'll all have to fit into the trunk along with my tools and the spare tire."

"What about the beds and the furniture?"

"Give them away."

"Can't we tie some of them on top of the car?"

I can just see us going down the road with all those damn cots and crappy dressers strapped on the top. What does she think this is--*The Grapes of Wrath*?

"No, Ma. We can't do that. It's a convertible."

"We'll need the knives and forks and my pressure cooker. The blankets and sheets. What about the pillows?"

"Take them. We can keep them up front to sleep on."

"No beds? No furniture? Where will we live?"

"We'll rent a furnished house."

"What about dishes and pans?"

"As soon as we get to Minnesota, we'll find a Salvation Army store so you can buy what you need."

"We'll have to find a doctor for Richie."

Acky comes out of the bathroom." I heard that--what's with this shit about moving? No way am I moving to Minnesota."

I say, "Great. We'll get better gas mileage without you in the car."

"I'm staying here."

"How're you gonna pay the rent?"

"I'll get a job."

"Doing what?"

"Plenty of jobs here."

"The employment agency don't have jobs for second story men."

Richie and Charley come out into the kitchen.

I say, "We're moving to Minnesota."

"No shit?" says Richie.

"That's the cat's ass," says Charley.

"Watch your language."

"Will we see wolves, Ma? Johnny said he saw wolves when he was there," says Richie.

Ma says, "They're probably not there any more."

Acky says, "They killed all the wolves, shot 'em. There's nothing left now but ice, snow and Eskimos."

"Ma, can I have the Indian Head pennies?" says Richie.

Charley says, "If we find 'em, we can split 'em up." Richie and Charley are nutso about the jar of Indian Head pennies Ma buried behind the barn when she was a little girl.

"We'll see," says Ma.

"Do they have Pepsi Cola there?" says Richie.

"When we get there, we'll see."

"But Ma, we could buy lotsa Pepsis with the pennies."

"Stop talking about Pepsi. Your teeth will fall out."

"What about the car? You'll never make it in that piece of shit," says Acky.

"It'll be OK."

"Are there horses on the farm?" says Richie.

"Remember when we rented horses in Central Park?" says Charley.

"Are we going in the Buick?" says Richie.

I say, "Yeah."

"Can we go with the top down?"

Acky says, "A convertible and you're going to Minnesota? You'll freeze your asses off."

"It's got a heater."

"The ragtop is shits. Didn't you say the frame was rusted and cracked?"

"It's been welded."

"I can see it now--the frame splits at eighty miles an hour, and Ma and the kids are splattered all over the highway, and the cops put you in jail."

"Knock it off."

Ma goes off to the closet, maybe to find a suitcase. I can hear her searching around. Acky's still dumping on me, but nobody's listening. Ma comes back with a shoe box and pulls out some photos.

"This is my mother standing in front of the barn--"

"Where the pennies are," says Richie.

"Look at the Model T on the right. I learned to drive on that."

"How come you don't drive any more, Ma?"

"That's a dumb question," says Acky. "Ma don't drive 'cause we have trolley cars and subways. You don't need a car in New York City."

"How come Johnny got a car?"

Acky says, "He uses it to pick up girls."

"Are they heavy?" says Charley. We all laugh.

"Johnny drives around looking for girls so he can get them in his car and do stuff to them."

"What kinda stuff?" says Charley.

"Like kissing?" says Richie.

Charley makes a face like sucking on a lemon. "Ugggh."

Richie says, "Is he gonna take them in the car when we go to Minnesota? I'm not going with no girls."

Richie loves girls. I know cause I see him with hard-ons every morning.

"No girls," I say. *Sure as shit, no girls.*

Richie looks into Ma's box and pulls out a penny. "Is this a Indian Head penny?"

Acky says, "Yeah, dummy, doncha see the Indian Head?"

"Axel, stop calling him a dummy."

Ma pulls out another picture and says, "This is our farmhouse. Those two boys on the porch are my brothers Axel and George."

"How come that one got the same name as Acky?"

"Your brother Axel was named after my brother Axel."

Acky hates his name. Wants everybody to call him Al, but nobody does.

Charley says, "Will we live in that house?"

"No, somebody else owns it now."

Then Ma looks into the shoe box like it was a crystal ball and starts talking about the past. Like how she had a lotta fun skiing in the woods and milking her favorite cow, Elsie. And how her and her brothers fixed up the old rattletrap Model T and drove to town for the first time. And how she saved Indian Head pennies for years in a glass jar and buried it behind the barn under a manure pile.

"Richie says, "You think the new owners found the pennies?"

1960 Hitting the Road

January

"Johnny. Watch out for the turnip truck."

"It's a potato truck."

"Turnips."

We've hit the road early. Richie, Charley and Ma are in the back. The radio's playing some cowboy crap about going on an Alaskan gold rush. Acky's up front with me, cooking up new ways to gripe.

> *North to Alaska*
> *They go north--the rush is on*
>
> *Big Sam left Seattle in the year of ninety-two*
> *With George Pratt, his partner, and brother Billy too.*
>
> *They crossed the Yukon River*
> *And found the Bonanza gold--*

All charged up, Richie and Charley are singing, following along with the radio. Ma's humming backup.

Me? I'm wondering what the hell I've done. We're in Jersey now--lots of factories, and the air stinks with the smell of sulphur and rubber, and I'm worried about the frame and the bald tire. *Hope the smell isn't Old Baldy coming apart.*

Richie says, "Ain't we going through Alaska?"

Acky says, "Good idea. We can go an extra two thousand miles, following the turnips and nuggets on the Yellow Brick Road."

Richie says, "Nuggets, nuggets."

Charley says, "I got a nugget." He pinches and twists one out of his nose, then proudly holds it up.

Acky says, "Hold it up in the sunlight so I can see the gold."

Ma says, "Stop that. It's disgusting."

Richie says, "What about the pennies?"

"Don't worry about them. Johnny's got it all covered. We'll be up to our necks in nuggets, pennies, and turnips."

Acky starts doing that sucking, clicking thing with his mouth--sorta like he has something stuck in his teeth and can't get it out. He knows how it pisses me off.

"Watch out, Johnny. There's a bouncing turnip."

"Where?" says Richie, "I don't see nothing."

I look at Acky's hands. I'm waiting to see that knuckle-popping shit. One finger at a time, he snaps them and gives me this "fuck you" look. *What an asshole.*

"I hafta go to the bathroom," says Charley.

"I'll stop at the next gas station."

"Can we get some Pepsis?" says Richie.

"Turnips--lots of 'em." Acky goes on with the turnip shit, trying to get a bug up my ass. His teeth sucking gets louder.

I say, "Do you have to do that?"

"What's the matter? You don't like turnips?"

"The teeth-sucking crap. Stop it."

"Let's make up a song about turnips," says Charley, bouncing around in his seat. "Turnips, turnips, yeah, yeah, yeah."

I say, "Stop jumping."

"That's right." says Acky. "You don't want Johnny's junker to split in half."

I say, "Why the hell did you bother coming with us? You coulda stayed on the block and slept in the alleys."

"Fuck you. Who made you boss?"

"Work, asshole. I went to work."

"Mickey Mouse stock boy. Call that a job?"

By now, I'm ready to stop the car and toss his ass out.

Ma sees I'm boiling and says, "Stop it. Can't you kids stop fighting?"

Richey says, "A forty-nine Chevy Deluxe Coupe."

Richie's got this cool way of changing the subject when a fight comes on. He starts doing his car ID thing. He may be scrambled eggs in the brain department, but when it comes to cars he's some kinda genius.

"Fifty-nine Ford Custom 300."

Acky says, "Knock it off. Enough about cars."

I'm worried about Richie. I look at him in the mirror and see his eyes looking funny.

"Ma," I say, "you got a good supply of pills for Richie?"

"Yes, John. I have the pills."

"Can we buy a sled when we get to Minnesota, Johnny?" says Charley.

"Better than that. I'll get you some skis and pull you through the woods on a ski-doo."

"What's a ski-doo?"

"It's sorta like a motorcycle that goes on snow."

"Fast?"

"Like fifty miles an hour."

"Will there be lakes?" says Richie.

"Ten thousand of them."

"How come you know that?"

"He counted them in his dreams," says Acky.

"It's on the license plates."

"When're we gonna stop? My ass is paralyzed," says Acky.

"I'm looking for a gas station."

"What's 'paralyzed' mean?" says Richie.

Acky says, "Like your head--numb, nothing moving--running on empty like this car."

"Ma, tell him my head's not empty."

"Stop making fun of your brother."

The sun is out, but I can't see it. I see nothing but smoke and factories. *Jesus, this part of Jersey is dirty. Why do they call it the Garden State?*

In the mirror, Ma smiles as she looks out the window, waiting for the smokestacks to turn into pine trees.

Made in the USA
Las Vegas, NV
03 September 2021